the power

of the invisible

The Power *of the* Invisible

Translated by GILBERT SHANG NDI

and ANA ISABEL VARGAS

University of New Mexico Press
Albuquerque

A Memoir of Solidarity,

Humanity, and Resilience

PAULA MORENO

ISBN 978-0-8263-6881-2 (paper)
ISBN 978-0-8263-6882-9 (ePub)

Library of Congress Control Number: 2025006824

Founded in 1889, the University of New Mexico sits on the traditional homelands of the Pueblo of Sandia. The original peoples of New Mexico—Pueblo, Navajo, and Apache—since time immemorial have deep connections to the land and have made significant contributions to the broader community statewide. We honor the land itself and those who remain stewards of this land throughout the generations and also acknowledge our committed relationship to Indigenous peoples. We gratefully recognize our history.

Cover image courtesy of Julián Gallo
Designed by Isaac Morris
Composed in Cochin, Dido LT, and Proxima Nova.

To Patty, my sister, in the silence of her evanescence.

Contents

Preface

"Paula, tell me about yourself." This simple yet profound request has echoed within me for nearly two decades, as if summoning the spirit of a distant, inscrutable figure—one whose essence eludes my grasp, yet whose story I am compelled to unravel. This journey has meant exposing myself in front of the mirror, both in solitude and in the company of others. I have examined my past from every angle, asking myself questions not only about the obvious things in my life, but also, and most important, about things I have long avoided seeing.

At twenty-eight I became both the first woman of African descent and the youngest person to serve as a minister in the history of Colombia. It is a country of nearly fifty million people, about ten million of whom are Black men and women, yet their role in the country's history has been confined to limited spheres—primarily music, dance, and sports. As valuable as these areas may be, stereotypes exclude Black Colombians from contributing in other fields such as economic development, politics, scientific research, or filmmaking. My appointment was unusual for one with neither a political past nor a family name with a pedigree. All this heightened the nature of the challenge. For people like me—those considered to be "different" and treated as "others"—the learning curve is often steeper, and patience from others scarcer. There is a constant need to explain, to justify, to answer the question: Why someone like you? And then the burden—and the pressure—of wanting to perform with excellence at any level. For me, it was triggered by the fear that what others consider negligible mistakes tend to be catastrophic when committed by a young Black woman.

Prior to my swearing in as minister, I searched for biographies of Black and young Latin American leaders with similar life paths. Unfortunately, I could find none. Thus, I understood the urgent need to reconstruct my story, writing it myself and sharing it with others, creating a chain of learning based on personal experiences. Stories, after all, are mirrors that reflect different truths. My story is not just my own; it is the common story of the millions of people considered as "marginalized" or "different" and the barriers they face in their quest for equality. My story is shared by those who dare to break preestablished rules and roles to assert that power must be exercised to build a more inclusive society.

My story remains that of men and women considered "different" who find themselves in positions of power: the first woman, the first Black person, the first Latino, the first of this or that, sometimes the "only representative" of a given group. Such exclusion is typical of identities that do not fit into the straitjacket created by a society bent on categorizing us: you people and us, whether it is based on race, gender, religion, orientation, or privilege. In short, it is a society that fails to consider difference as something natural and normal, as something deserving care and respect. Acknowledging our shared humanity thanks to our differences and not in spite of them remains a utopian dream, an exception to the rule.

The world today is caught in between progressive and regressive trends, between those trying to dismantle exclusion and those hanging on to historical paradigms that keep some people subordinate. Amid these tensions, I believe it is more than ever worthwhile to personalize stories that give meaning to causes and dare us to believe, once again, that human dignity is possible.

Writing this book has been therapeutic for me, as well as for my family, friends, and many across more than thirty countries that have been part of it. This story has been written and rewritten, and it shall continue to evolve as I, with your aid, come to grasp more fully the art of wielding power from unconventional paths. Speaking about the self is never easy, but I have learned that life only truly blossoms into deeper meaning when one traces the intricate tapestry of our experiences.

This memoir was originally published in 2018. Now, as we prepare to launch this new English-language edition, it is time to reflect on the experiences and insights gained during this transformative eight-year journey. Over these years, I have witnessed the ever-growing representation of women, particularly Black women, across all spheres of contemporary life—from the arts and academia to the private sector and political arena.

These are groundbreaking times as identities begin to challenge and reshape entrenched power structures.

When I first wrote this book, the invisibility of Black women was palpable; invisibility is not merely an absence, it is a cultural strategy to maintain power and decision-making control while exerting coercion. Today, our visibility and agency have undeniably increased, even amid systemic bias. As I worked on this updated version, I was profoundly moved by the growing influence of women, especially Black women. We are witnessing a shift that challenges the status quo, yet the crucial question remains: Are we genuinely changing the rules? This shared, diversified power is an ongoing experiment, marked by incremental progress but, regrettably, significant backlash. In the final chapter of this revised edition, I will explore the nuances of this evolving representation, examining whether it has led to tangible social and systemic change and whether it has wielded influence effectively. After all, just because "we" are now at the helm, does that guarantee a different outcome? The answer appears to be an ambiguous "yes and no." This is the challenge we face—a social learning process striving for increasing representational diversity, set against the complex and polarized landscape of identity politics.

I invite you, dear reader, to join me in navigating this landscape as we delve into the intricate power dynamics that shape the experiences of women and young people. We stand at the threshold of a transformative era, one that courageously challenges the status quo. This memoir is not just a reflection of the past, it also is a beacon illuminating the path forward, urging us to harness the transformative power that arises from reclaiming visibility and agency. Together, let us ignite a movement that reshapes our understanding of identity and representation and fosters a relentless pursuit of equity for all.

Part I

The Mystery of a Ministry

It was the first day of June 2007. The time had come for me to be sworn in as minister. One hour before the ceremony, I was joined by my family, my longtime friends, two leaders from the women's movement and community councils from the Pacific region, several ambassadors, and some of my mentors. We were about fifty people gathered in one of the rooms of the Casa de Nariño (the Presidential Palace), a rectangular space with a dark wooden caoba floor, cream-colored walls with white moldings. The room featured a large mirror at the back that reflected the entire space, creating an illusion of openness, along with several large windows that allowed soft, natural light to fill the area. The guests had formed an honor guard, and at the end of the room, a red carpet nearly covered the entire floor. On one side stood a tripod with two microphones—one for the presenter and one for the president.

A week before, my mother told me, "This is a once-in-a-lifetime event. We cannot afford to improvise." She reached out to our friends, who referred us to a very elegant boutique in one of Bogota's most luxurious fashion districts. Armed with all our credit cards, we went to meet this designer. Although his proposed attire cost nearly half my salary, it was deemed appropriate for the occasion. I ended up wearing a green dress that gave me peace and brightness, but which made me look more like an elderly lady. In his opinion, a minister always needed to look like someone elderly, and he did just that.

President Álvaro Uribe and First Lady Lina Moreno arrived, hand in hand, walking briskly. Lady Lina, as she was called by many, was nearly running to keep up with him. She was a slim woman of average height, with short dark hair, always discreet, simple, and elegant. On that day, she wore low-heel black shoes, black slacks, a white blouse, and a black cashmere coat. As soon as they entered, they greeted each guest on their way to the front, where my mother, my sister Patricia, my aunt Cecilia, and my friend Carmen Cecilia were seated, close to me. The President and First Lady took their seats and invited me to sit in the middle, between them and the presenter. The resolution was read, I took the oath, and they welcomed me warmly. In just ten minutes, the ceremony was over. It was my first induction ceremony, and I had imagined delivering a speech like those presidents do in television broadcasts. I had envisioned myself reading words that felt like a piece of my heart. Yet, when the moment arrived, I found myself unable to share it, as it was not part of the protocol. Those carefully chosen words remained unspoken, but they are forever treasured in my memory.

Chapter 1

Induction Speech

First and foremost, I wish to thank God for granting me this opportunity. I pray that He fills me with His infinite wisdom, unwavering love, and unshakable strength. My appointment marks a historical threshold that transcends my humble self; it represents the aspirations of the nation's youths, women, and ethnic communities.

Throughout history, culture has often been the invisible hand driving societal progress, the force behind development and social cohesion in times of crisis. It has been the matrix of a nationalism that fosters interconnectivity with the global community.

My commitment is to all Colombian people. I recognize the gravity of my historic mission, and I grasp it with unwavering confidence, for I know that through our differences, we can each contribute significantly to the consolidation of a society that reflects us all and provides opportunity for everyone.

The ceremony was so brief that I was left with the impression of a television reality show. Was it going to be possible for me to be myself without feeling that I was being filmed all the time, and to what effect?

As soon as it was over, I walked a hundred yards across the street to the seat of the Ministry of Culture, El Palacio Echeverri, a neoclassical structure at the corner of the street. The public entrance, originally designed as an entrance for the cleaning personnel, gave the impression of an institution with restricted access. One of the first things I did as minister was to request that the entrance be changed, as I wanted my tenure to be remembered as an open-door ministry. As I surveyed the space, I noticed the absence of plants, which led me to envision the ambiance I wanted to create, one that would bring warmth to this cold traditional heritage palace.

My office was a rectangular room with a high ceiling, decorated with green paintings and white moldings. It was furnished with rather classical pieces. I asked for a large map of Colombia to be placed on the wall in front of my desk, as I needed to focus on the country as a whole to better understand the intricacies of its geography. In these first moments, what truly delighted me in that space was the presence of a sound system; I knew I would need music. And so I began to breathe life into the space, gradually filling it with the gifts received during my visits to the most remote corners of the country or sent to my office as souvenirs. I wanted the office to be filled with the wishes, the desires, and the affection of the communities we served, so that every time I looked around, I would be reminded of a promise, a sense of gratitude that would provide meaning and motivation.

Chapter 2

The Experiment

The days went by, and with each passing moment I felt that this whole endeavor was just an experiment. My role as minister seemed unnatural, even unreal, to almost everyone. Many, both within the ministry and the government, felt that this was an endeavor doomed to fail in the coming months. Some did not even bother to hide their doubts. At times, the disdain was so palpable that individuals would not deign to offer even the simplest greeting. At first, everything was mired in complication—the most effortless processes now burdened with unusual delays. It all seemed deliberately orchestrated to make me and my team feel like unwelcome interlopers. We were seen as nothing more than temporary intruders.

The first meeting, where we were introduced to the outgoing minister, said it all. We entered the office of the secretary general at the presidency, who was responsible for the introduction. I greeted her with a "Good day, madam." She looked at me from head to toe and said, "Paula, you are so young!" Her surprise was evident. She was an elderly woman, highly esteemed for her service as Director of the National Museum and as a representative of the ruling conservative party. The transition meeting began with courtesy but was tinged with subtle tension. We assigned the details of the transition process to our respective teams and only met twice in person.

For the cultural sector of the capital Bogotá, my arrival was unwelcome with palpable distrust. "You do not know who I am?" several renowned artists queried, their offense clear when I admitted my ignorance. How could someone unfamiliar with them assume this role? In contrast, the regional cultural spheres responded with solidarity and collaboration, celebrating my appointment as a step toward inclusion. This ministerial post seemed to be an experiment—both for the skeptical city and the welcoming provinces.

I recall being introduced to one of Colombia's renowned musicians: "Meet Paula, the Minister of Culture." The artist pulled me aside, brow furrowed. "Minister of Culture, from where? From which African country?" He had to be told twice that I was from Colombia—for a Black minister in our nation was an anomaly.

Facing such public challenges alone proved immensely difficult in those early days. I turned to my mentors for advice, including Malcolm Deas, a professor at Oxford, who wrote to me saying:

> Dear Paula,
>
> I wish you all the best and would like to offer some advice.
>
> Remember to take up this task with prudence, honesty, transparency and hold on to your family and to people closest to you, many new friends will appear but rely on those who have been with you from the beginning.
>
> Get yourself a good lawyer and do not sign any document without his revision.
>
> Be cautious in your interactions with journalists.
>
> Do not become absorbed or distracted by daily comments or happenings, be selective on what deserves your attention.
>
> Always give yourself some space to develop and prioritize what will be your legacy.

A group of leaders and friends fought to ensure this "experiment" would succeed. In the beginning, they called daily to check on my progress, rallying cultural figures to lend support. They accompanied me to events, offered recommendations, and issued warnings whenever they sensed a potential threat. This leap of faith—in intentions beyond myself, aimed at empowering those like me—provided comfort and hope. Life then was a tumultuous mix of emotion and anxiety. The priority after my appointment was to marshal all resources to meet the challenge, focusing on effective management and quick results to refute the disqualifying claims of the detractors. I learned to rely on my own faculties—my skills and work ethic. This was not about posturing or hastily becoming an expert on cultural affairs. I had two weeks before the induction ceremony to map out the ministry, its challenges and priorities. My background as an industrial engineer aided in analyzing the organization, its processes, and focal points to ensure effective management. The crucial step was defining our management approach, which benefited immensely from the contributions of three friends with complementary public, private, and academic expertise. This collaborative effort resulted in the document "Diverse Colombia: Culture of All, Culture for All." I worked on it early in the morning, while at night we would gather in one of our apartments to finalize it. It served as our roadmap, outlining expected results and measurable goals. For me it was crucial to arrive on the first day with my agenda to avoid leaving what I wanted to achieve open to interpretation. Building upon existing frameworks, it recentered the axes of diversity and inclusion.

From day one, with so many distractions, we had to lead a team, align the sector, to the contribution we wanted to make and develop the strategy to execute. At first, everything seemed important, and maybe it was, but there was simply no way to address every issue, opportunity, or problem, or to deliver on everything. I was focused on the legacy I wanted to leave and wrote in my journal: "I want to be remembered as a good, serious, rigorous, hard-working, and calm minister who demonstrated with results how the power of diversity enriches our country as a whole. That's why I'm here."

Chapter 3

How It All Started

"*Do you want to serve our country?* Tell me about your family."

This was the question that President Alvaro Uribe Velez asked just a few seconds after meeting me in early May 2007.

It was a day just like any other in Bogotá. I woke up early and took my breakfast my mom had prepared for me, even though I was twenty-eight. She had recently retired and thus had all the time to indulge my cravings—some banana chips with cheese and fresh juice, all I needed to start the day. I spent the morning finishing the first part of a report for a development agency consultancy, then headed off to a meeting to validate its content.

I was driving my new car—the first I ever had—heading for the Pan-American Health Organization where I had been hired to analyze the exclusion of ethnic communities in Colombia from healthcare services. My work involved a series of case studies on principal diseases among the population, the majority of which were Black and Indigenous communities of the Colombian Amazon and the Pacific coast. The main aim was to come out with an x-ray of the structural factors that keep part of the population ill, especially children and women, and how a lack of access to essential services was often tied to structural racism. It was very interesting to note the relationship between the lack of potable water and the few medical professionals who understood the cultural specificities and the prevalent prejudices. I felt that these failings were almost intentional, and this was part of the message I wanted to bring to the table at that meeting.

As soon as I entered the car and turned the key in the ignition, I put on a collection of my favorite salsa music that usually boosted my energy and filled me with happiness for the rest of the day. I sang and tapped the steering wheel, nodding my head to the rhythm—forward to mark the beat and sideways along to the changes—as if it were a drum. That was like a ritual to me. However, on that day, I was forced to stop my car at a corner and to reduce the volume. My phone had been ringing without me noticing, and when I finally checked, I saw several missed calls from the same number. This was clearly urgent. I called back immediately: the President of the Republic wanted to meet me at twelve thirty, and it was already noon. I hung up and pulled into the nearest parking lot. I was so nervous that I chose to take a taxi to the city center, my heart pounding with anticipation. As the city whizzed by outside the window, I couldn't shake the overwhelming thought of meeting the most powerful person in the country—someone I had only ever seen on television. A mixture of excitement and anxiety coursed through me; I felt like a character in a surreal narrative, stepping into a world that had always felt distant and unattainable. Each passing landmark reminded me of the gravity of the moment ahead, and I wondered if I would be able to convey my thoughts clearly or if my nerves would betray me.

The previous day, I had been in the office of the private secretary of the presidency for an interview. It was my first time in Casa de Nariño, which, like most Colombians, I had only seen from afar, usually from Bolivar Square, whenever I visited the Primatial Cathedral of Bogotá, a few blocks away. At the gate, I handed in my identity card and left my phone behind before a young soldier escorted me along a small, silver-plated elevator. Once on the second floor, we walked along a small labyrinth, still on the red carpet, with secretaries looking at me from every corner of the offices. We then reached the door of the secretary's office where we were received by her aide.

The private secretary greeted me from the preserve of her office. She kept quiet for a few minutes as she glanced down at my CV, holding it in one hand while adjusting the red frame of her small rectangular eyeglasses with the other. She told me they were looking for a Black woman for an important government position, though she did not specify which. She looked at me from the corner of her eye and started asking me a series of questions about my experience, my worldview, and my contacts. She was undoubtedly from the Caribbean, judging from the musicality of her voice and the confidence in her way of speaking, as well as from the color of her nails, her makeup, and her attire: a printed jacket on top of a yellow blouse. She was a rather slim lady, with an indecipherable look. I recall having told her in the latter part of our conversation that I was a woman with a strong character, using the word *quilichagueño*; that is, typical of women from my hometown who taught me to live by and for my principles: frank, rigorous, and persistent. In front of the secretary, I felt composed and secure. I don't know why, but I wanted to make it clear to her that I had well-defined and clear goals and purpose. Since they didn't know me, and I didn't know them, I was determined to establish my presence. The only thing the secretary (a distant, executive, and rather blunt woman) said was, "We do not need silly people around here, people without standards."

At the end, she told me she was in the process of evaluating the interviewed candidates. Then she added the customary polite phrase about letting me know once she had made her decisions. I thanked her and thought to myself that she had at least left the door open for some new opportunities like, maybe, some consultancies. I found it difficult to deduce what kind of impression I had made. There was no expression of sympathy from her. Only a "See you later," which I could not tell if it meant "See you never" or "See you soon."

That is what was on my mind when the taxi driver dropped me close to the Casa de Nariño for me to meet the president. The time was 12:25 p.m. It was then that I realized I was in my casual attire of a young consultant: denim slacks, a shirt, low heels, and my handbag. Being twenty-eight years old, I thought such attire was formal enough working in the field of international development. But upon entering the presidential palace, I realized how much I needed to be in high heels and much more appropriate wear. It was a different context.

In any case, I went in, breathed deeply, prayed earnestly, and finally stepped into the hall with two leather sofas and white wooden seats with red cushions. I did not sit down or even take in my surroundings, apart from looking at the window, wondering, "What will he ask me?" "What should I say?" But in the back of my mind, I was shouting, "Oh my God, why am I here?"

There was no one in this space but me. More so, I knew just nobody in this center of power. Some minutes later, one of the presidential aides informed me that the head of state was about to arrive. It took only seconds for Álvaro Uribe to arrive. As soon as he stepped into the light-filled room, he greeted me warmly, saying, "Daughter, to begin with, how are you?"

The term "daughter"—or *hija* in Spanish—is a colloquial expression that conveyed warmth and highlighted my youth in relation to my position.

He stretched his hand to me and asked me two questions. He wanted to know who my parents were and whether I would like to serve the country. I told him about my parents, and without hesitation, I said, "Of course, I want to serve." He started moving from one corner of the room to the other, outlining his priorities for national cultural programs, focusing on expanding the coverage of cultural goods and services such as books and music. Then he left suddenly, without saying goodbye. In the space of a second, I took a deep breath. I did not know what had happened but . . . well, alright. . . . That was until the president, in the middle of the corridor facing the room, met with his press secretary and said to him in a clear and firm voice, "Please, pass on the announcement that she is our new Minister of Culture. And remember to call a press conference." And he walked away without looking back, without even asking for my input or waiting for a response.

Maybe he noticed that if he did, with the level of astonishment and nervousness I felt and could not control, God alone knows what my answer would have been. During our encounter, I responded with as few words as possible, and my entire body spoke of tension. I did not move a step. That was the president, a decisive man, one who did not consult further whenever he knew what he really wanted.

I was in shock for a few seconds. The sunlit room suddenly seemed huge, and I could not stop wondering if this was really happening to me, because I had never imagined being in such a situation. Two members of the presidential staff came into the room and asked me if I needed to call anyone. I responded, "Yes, please!" They immediately brought my cell phone, which I had left at the gate. I took it into my trembling hands and slipped out onto a balcony to call my mom.

"Mamá," I said, "I have just been appointed Minister; look what I got myself into!" But my mother's response was perfectly calm, without a hint of emotion. "The news is already out on TV," she assured me. "God won't give you more than you can handle. You're no more or less than anyone else. We'll talk later." And with that, she hung up. It was clear she knew this was no time for lengthy discussion or analysis—only action. I had expected my mother to be overjoyed, but she met the news with composure, even a certain coldness. Yet she understood, from experience and faith, that even with God's help, the road ahead would not be easy.

Leaving the room, I saw many people, but I did not look at any of them. All I can remember was walking down the corridor wanting to immediately go home and change my clothes. I passed in front of an office where I met an Afro-descendant congressman from the state of Chocó who called to me and said, sounding disappointed, "So, now you are the minister?" I stopped to greet him, but he did not hold out his hand to me. He just looked at me with contempt and said, "I cannot understand why they appointed you; you do not represent us." I only recall giving him my hand once more, saying, "Thank you and see you later." I looked down like someone wanting to be totally oblivious to that moment, switched on my autopilot, and continued moving, hoping that no one was looking at me or was going to say anything to me as I walked. I needed to start building up my armor.

Chapter 4

The First and the Only One

In 2006, I began teaching courses to first and last semester students on the role of engineering in development and the phenomenon of globalization. On Saturdays, my day started at seven in the morning and ended at one o'clock in the afternoon at the Autonomous University, located at the heart of the historical center of the city. It was the same institution where I had earned my degree in industrial engineering. After my classes, I would walk to the corner of the university, half a block to the north, and have lunch at the Secrets of the Sea—a restaurant that truly lived up to its name. The stairs were narrow and the wood worn and creaky; the entire restaurant was painted in baby blue, evoking the Pacific Ocean, with murals that portrayed the floor of those rivers that emptied into the sea between the mountains, those coves of green olive water, hemmed in by rocks. It was a space where accents from the coast mingled, and we could enjoy familiar dishes like soups, seafood, and fish prepared with traditional herbs. Not to mention the *marimba* and *chirimía* music genres that were not common in radio stations in Bogotá. Its owner, Jesus Aboni, known to everyone as Chucho, was a nice guy with frizzy, black, short hair, slim stature, average height, with three braids on his chin and a bright smile, large and black eyeballs that grew larger whenever he was greeting you, just like mine. His presence and the way he welcomed us made Secrets of the Sea feel like home.

It was in that quaint restaurant that I first crossed paths with Andrés Palacios and Giovanny Córdoba, two spirited young men from Chocó whom many had urged me to meet, especially since we had all recently returned from our studies abroad. This place soon became our cherished gathering spot, a vibrant backdrop for the conversations and camaraderie that would deepen our bonds and shape our journeys—Andrés having completed his doctorate in Germany, while Giovanni and I had earned our master's in England. It was Giovanni who arranged our first meeting, and from the start, we found a kinship in our way of speaking and mannerisms, but most important, in our shared quests.

Once a week, I had lunch with these two tall, elegant young men—the most sought-after bachelors of the time. I always found us seated around the same wooden table in the corner of the second-floor attic space, having climbed the narrow staircase, crouching slightly with the ceiling just a few inches above my head. Our usual order included fish stew, rice, plantain, and a refreshing glass of *agua de panela* with lemon. It was here that we came to realize that just as this restaurant remained invisible and unnoticed by most in the city center, so too was our presence as a Black community often overlooked in the country. At the very least, we needed to start changing the narrative by becoming visible and fostering connections among one another.

Though I was the youngest at twenty-six, with both Andrés and Giovanni already in their thirties, we shared the bond of being part of the first wave of Black professionals who benefited from scholarships to study at elite universities and to work in renowned institutions, but we were acutely aware of the fact that—beyond our academic and technical domains—we were meant to play a significant public role in our community. We always met in that same space. Narrow and small as it was, it was ours.

Sometime later, Andrés was appointed advisor and then Director of Promotion in the Ministry of Social Protection. Through this role he came in contact with the president of the Republic, who at the end of 2006 asked him to recommend the curriculum vitae of Black women for an executive position in his administration. Without telling me, Andrés put forth my candidature and told the president that I was polyglot and had expertise in international cooperation and academia, and that I was someone he knew and trusted. When he called me to ask for my resume, my first reaction was, "I do not see myself in it, and I do not want to go down in flames." I had never thought of working with the government nor harbored any political ambitions, except if it was something of a diplomatic position. Neither did I belong to any political party nor entertained close ties with any politician of any leaning. Andrés insisted for weeks. Even if I was confident of my training and sense of discipline, I was not sure if I was up to the task. In

April 2007, he told me the President had not yet found the right candidate and he was again after me: "Dear Paula, just send me your resume. That is all I am asking." I finally agreed to give adequate thought to it and make a few inquiries. I meant it. I called my mentor in Oxford, Malcolm Deas, to ask him if he honestly thought I could handle this. He knew the president, having been his professor at Oxford University. In addition, he had worked for almost fifty years as advisor of several Colombian presidents and taught a considerable number of the country's top cadres. Malcolm's response was encouraging. I sent in my resume.

Chapter 5

Where Does She Come From?

In the whirlwind of my new role, a multitude of anecdotes surfaced as people learned of my appointment. One of the most memorable involved my aunt Cecilia, when she saw the news on TV in her house in our hometown, Santander de Quilichao (Cauca). Overwhelmed by emotion, she ran out into the street to break the good news to her neighbors. She saw my cousins show up at the corner. One of them, who was returning home, limping and feeling dizzy after a medical checkup, noticed my aunt at the front door of the house, screaming, "Paula has been appointed, Paula has been appointed!" But my cousins were astonished because they misheard her and thought she was screaming "Paula has been assassinated, Paula has been assassinated!" and took my aunt's leaping as a sign of distress. And so, my limping cousin ran toward the house to inquire what the matter was. When they reached the house, my aunt, with tears in her eyes and with great emotion that was quite unusual of her, clarified her announcement, "No . . . I mean she has been appointed Minister!"

The day after the announcement, I was back in the classroom at seven o'clock in the morning, teaching my Globalization and Development course to my fifty students at the Autonomous University. That morning I woke up at the usual time, but as I was leaving the parking lot, a gentleman approached me, introducing himself as a police officer assigned to accompany me prior to my induction. I thanked him but politely declined and let him know that I would rather go alone. Some fifteen minutes later, as I was driving to the university, when I stopped at one of the traffic lights, I realized with astonishment that people stuck their necks out of taxis and private cars, whistling and waving at me. After coming out of my class and walking to my car, everyone was greeting me on the street. At that moment, I felt a sense of disquiet. I became conscious that I was no longer anonymous. Not to mention my last class in which many students, beaming with pride, looked at me, saying, "You did not tell us about this!" "Take care, professor!" I enjoyed teaching, and with this particular group, I entertained a rather special relationship. So on that day, feeling their support, their genuine joy and confidence meant the world to me, especially as I was still coming to terms with the life-altering changes ahead.

The phones in our house never stopped ringing—my cell phone but also my mother's. In less than two days, we had no choice but to change our phone numbers. We received calls from people we had not spoken to in years, from college classmates to my kindergarten teachers, all reaching out to confirm that the Paula Marcela they knew was indeed the new Minister.

The announcement of my appointment triggered a huge reaction—as well as euphoria and media exposure—that left me totally astounded. Overnight, I became a target for interviews from major journalists and landed on the front pages of the tabloids. Suddenly, everyone wanted to have lunch with me and talk to me, even people I knew nothing about. Out of the blue, I became a public figure, and with time, I became increasingly aware of how much my life had changed.

Two of my best friends, Tina Song and Rosa Andújar (two New Yorkers, daughters of Taiwanese and Dominican immigrants respectively), with whom I studied at Cambridge University, read the news in the *New York Times* and in BBC, respectively. On seeing my name, they wrote to me to inquire if by chance I was the one in question.

When Tina wrote to me, saying, "I just read the article in the *New York Times*. Paula, are you the new Colombian Minister of Culture they are talking about?" my response was, "Dear Tina, you cannot imagine how one's life can change in just a second." The note in the *New York Times* was an article examining the humanitarian crisis caused by the drug wars in Buenaventura, the main port of the country, with close to ninety percent Black population. At the end of the article, the correspondent made a brief reflection on the situation of the Afro-Colombian population and on how my appointment came as a result of international pressure from the Congressional Black Caucus of the United States in favor of Black representation in the Colombian government. Despite my appointment, the situation in Buenaventura has not changed—a paradox in which one of the country's main ports, through which goods are shipped and distributed in thousands of containers to other parts of the world, reflects nothing of this abundance and welfare. In this place, populated mostly by Black and poor people, wealth flows indifferently, while the growing discomfort of its inhabitants increases as they demand a redistribution of the benefits, because it is not a port without people. The BBC article, forwarded to me by my friend Rosa, was titled "Colombia Towards Racial Integration," and brought together views from both academics and political leaders to analyze the implications of my appointment. One of them posited that my appointment was more for the sake of Afro-Americans than it was for Afro-Colombians. This claim—repeated not only in those initial days but indeed during the entire period of my tenure as minister—was something I responded to by asserting that the African diaspora constituted a strong force of global solidarity. That we are more than 1.5 billion Africans and their descendants who have for centuries maintained this umbilical cord with our ancestral land and a negritude which, no matter where we find ourselves, defines our being in the world. Africa and its lineage live in me and in the reality of more than 10 million Afro-Colombians and more than 150 million Afro-Latinos. This collective consciousness that traces itself to Africa accompanies us everywhere, even if we do not know for sure which specific part of the continent we come from. Without doubt, I was the result of that fraternity, that project of affinity. I was a member of that mental and emotional community, which, even without speaking the same language, shares a common agenda and a joint transnational struggle to give new meaning to its existence, humanity, and dignity.

The visible representation of Afro-Colombians in the cabinet signaled to the world that Black communities in Colombia not only exist but are significant, representing the second largest African diaspora presence in Latin America after Brazil. I was thrilled to know that my appointment would spark renewed collective claims and displays of strength within our community.

In August 2007, during my first visit to Washington following my appointment, we first celebrated in the office of US Congressman Gregory Meeks, the great leader of the Afro-Colombian agenda in Washington, and thereafter in the office of another congressman, Charles Rangel, together with his team. These were special moments for me, for they made me know that the members of the Congressional Black Caucus were very delighted with my appointment. I was left with the assurance that they were going to lend me their support during my tenure. In fact, they constituted my political backing.

Next in line to express its support was the academic sector through the board of trustees of the Association for the Study of the Worldwide African Diaspora (ASWAD), as well as the cultural sector through the board of the Smithsonian's National Museum of African American History and Culture. Not only in the United States but also in Brazil, the headlines also reflected this momentum. I vividly recall that the first calls and letters I received were from the renowned singer-songwriter Gilberto Gil, who was then the first Afro-Brazilian Minister of Culture. In the first two weeks of my appointment, he invited me to Brazil and some months after, paid me a return visit in Colombia. From day one, he offered the support of his management team, and together we launched numerous programs. As two of the few Afro-Latino ministers of culture, we were acutely aware of the significance of our roles. Gilberto became my mentor and inspiration, profoundly influencing my approach as minister. I resonated with his perspectives on cultural diversity, the democratization of cultural goods and services, and the vision of culture as a focal point for development.

Gilberto introduced me to a Brazil that was both familiar and foreign, fostering a strong and affectionate partnership that blossomed into friendship. When I first met him, he was a slender man with a deep, penetrating gaze framed by thick eyelids and large, expressive eyes that conveyed a blend of strength, perceptiveness, and tenderness. His presence radiated tranquility and wisdom, and the tone of his voice flowed in harmony with his thoughts. His broad smile, dark hair speckled with white, and braided locks added to his striking stature. Gilberto was, to me, a beacon of light, much like "Farolito," a song by Agustín Lara that he dedicated to me during his last concert in Colombia. As the lyrics suggest, he was the little streetlamp that illuminated my desolate street, guiding me through the complexities of our shared cultural management journey.

Two years later, I had another remarkable experience with Simão Souindoula, the Director of the Museum of Slavery in Angola. He visited

Cartagena as part of the Afro-descendant Agenda in the Americas, a program I had organized to connect cultural leaders from Africa and the diaspora, fostering transnational cultural policy exchanges. Simão presented me with an Angolan newspaper bearing the headline, "Angolan Appointed as Minister in Colombia," alongside another daily from another country that identified me as "A Bantu Minister." He also gifted me a large, solid wooden carving of an African sage, explaining that it symbolized the wisdom of our ancestors, meant to accompany me in all my endeavors. Africa was a priority for me, and whenever the opportunity arose—be it in Paris or Washington—I seized the chance to connect with African ambassadors and leaders. My message was clear: we were part of a small fragment of Africa scattered across Colombia, and this reunion held profound meaning for us. Even though I did not know exactly which part of the continent my ancestors might have come from, it was at some point suggested to me that I was from Congo, Nigeria, or the Ivory Coast. Years later, when I visited Mali, I was warmly embraced as one of their own. In essence, I held dual citizenship: both as a Colombian and as an Afro-descendant.

As I continued to make international contacts, days and weeks passed and the question on everyone's lips was, "Where does she come from?" wanting to know more about my life story with a mixture of curiosity, support, and affection. Some of the headlines and columns in the Colombian press ranged from "Add Some Color to This Country," "Black Reengineering in the Ministry of Culture," "Blanquita," to "Black Cinderella." For about a month, a caricaturist from one of the major national newspapers unleashed a series of damning and racist depictions of me. In one particularly hurtful illustration, I was portrayed as a woman with grotesquely exaggerated lips, frozen in a bewildered expression that suggested total cluelessness. The image was further distorted by bulging eyes gazing up at a commanding white hand, reducing me to a caricature of ignorance—an individual with little understanding of the world around her. This portrayal was not merely a personal affront; it also represented a well-trodden path in the depiction of Black people in Colombia, a narrative that persists even today.

My appointment was based on a reality that was new to many in the country: the representativeness of diverse groups in positions of power, Black men and women, Indigenous and young people who only count as voters and consumers in the statistics, but never as people qualified for top leadership. This prompted questions like: Was this participation a matter of right, duty, or undue privilege? Is it to say that more than ten million people do not deserve to partake in leadership at the national level?

My appointment triggered a series of questions: "Why was she appointed? By virtue of her being Black or because she deserves it? And given that she is Black, is she going to govern and lead only for her own community?" I also encountered a patronizing attitude that drew a clear line between "us" as "you, the others" who are not part of us, as if we were an infection, an unwelcome presence. For example, a prominent columnist provocatively asked, "Where did the president get the idea of choosing such a young and inexperienced woman of color?" This statement was not just a question, it also was a loaded remark that resonated with a pervasive skepticism in the public's mind. It seemed to signify that my identity alone overshadowed my qualifications, disregarding the fact that my resume, at the very least, was on par with—if not superior to—that of my predecessors. Such sentiments reflected a deep-seated bias, casting doubt on my abilities simply because of who I was. Another columnist, this time the director of the main cultural review of Bogotá, reacted to my appointment with an opinion piece titled "The Point Is Not That of Race," which claimed to be concerned not with my blackness but rather my age and the fact that I knew nothing of culture since I was not from any of the elite families. Thus, her prediction was that "I was going to hit the rocks" and that the country's cultural sector was in total distress.

In the same culture magazine, the opinion column that analyzed my appointment was titled "Blanquita." In Colombia, Blanquita was the only Black character in an advertisement for the sale of laundry bleach. It referred to the Black woman who cleans everything white. For decades, it was thought that this was all that we were good at. Unfortunately, the said column did not acknowledge the role of Black women who served in various positions, nor the domestic workers and their contribution to the country's families and social welfare. All that it was interested in was: "What is black? Are there so many here? Is it that they exist but we do not know about them? Why are they black and not white with dark skin? Do they have a certain dignity that the nation needs to respect? Would the new minister be critical or merely a stooge?" To think that Black women, often used as decoration to market products or in touristic campaigns affixed to a static role in society, would now acquire an independent voice and power was something deeply unsettling, too complicated to be understood and accepted. Amid the barrage of negativity, I also found a wellspring of support. Eduardo Posada Carbo, an Oxford University academic with whom I met when I was a student in Cambridge, wrote at the end of one of his weekly columns in *El Tiempo*: "I know Paula Moreno, I acknowledge her capacities, and I think the country needs to give her this chance." This message was very important as it weighed in against the negative and racist press coverage that had begun to poison the environment for me.

Another article titled "The Black Cinderella" addressed the issue of justice regarding Black communities. It acknowledged the necessary, undeniable, and unwavering contribution of the Afro-Colombian population that claimed its place in society. As I read it, I could not help but ponder, "How is it possible to move from a centuries-old struggle whereby one is considered nobody to be somebody?" Although, to make things clear, it is not the story of the maidservant who meets her charming prince, nor that of the poor who becomes rich. Rather, it was about a relentless struggle to normalize what society still deemed exceptional due to class, race, gender, or any particular identity.

In a personal profile article, a reporter marveled at my story. I responded, "Colombia has always been a country of peasants who, like my grandmother, laid the groundwork for the development we enjoy today. I am certain that in ninety percent of Colombian ancestries, you will find someone like my grandmother. So why does it sound extraordinary when I acknowledge that truth?" My words sought to illuminate the often-overlooked contributions of ordinary lives, challenging the narrative that places value solely on the extraordinary.

A group of academics and ethnic activists created blogs with a series of questions such as: "How will Paula exercise power? Will she be just like any woman or will she exercise power with the sensibility of someone who knows from lived experiences what it means to be excluded? "

For more than two weeks, I became exposed to so much media buzz that I felt like I had been turned into an exotic exhibition of someone considered different. So, I decided to call off the show. I resolved to speak only about my ministry and not about my personal life or identity. Just the ministry and nothing else. After all, that is what I was appointed for.

Part II

In the Shadow of the Saman

Since I was about six or seven years old, during the 1980s, I vividly remember the evening of the last day of school. My mother and my aunt packed my suitcase alongside those of my cousins, Emelías and Patricia, as we prepared for our journey from Bogotá to Santander de Quilichao. Before we headed to the transport terminal, they carefully listed the dos and don'ts for the two months we would spend with Aunt Cecilia, the eldest sister and matriarch of our family.

Santander de Quilichao is a small quaint town that defines my childhood. The journey we used to make from Bogotá to Santander twice a year, in June and before Christmas, was a homecoming, a return to our cradle, for my cousins and me. Though we were born in Bogotá, Santander was ever-present in our minds, kept alive by the daily reminiscence of the hometown expressed by my aunt Nidia and my mother, who had settled in the city in the sixties. We usually left Bogotá at night, only to wake up in the bus eight or nine hours later, at the crack of dawn, when the countryside was converted into a valley carpeted by vegetation and sugarcane plantations, with the cordillera rising in the background through the window of the intermunicipal bus. We were filled to the brim. To us, this vegetation meant a different breath, full of life and liberty.

Thirty miles from the city of Cali is Santander de Quilichao, home to about eighty thousand people. The city's origins date back to 1543, when the Spanish conquistador Sebastian de Belalcazar named it "Jamaica of the Quilichaos," drawing comparisons to the island he had visited on an earlier expedition. The name was later changed in 1827 to honor the independence hero Francisco de Paula Santander. The Indigenous Quilichaos, who once inhabited the land, referred to it as the "Land of Gold." This was a reference not only to the region's mineral wealth but also to the fertility of its soil. The town has long been known as the "City of the Samans," a reference to the colossal, shade-giving trees that line the banks of the local river. Residents would gather to talk, and children would play among the towering roots. In the shadow of the samans, I always felt that nothing better represented the symbol of eternity: immense and millennial.

Santander de Quilichao is woven with the threads of Indigenous, Black, and Mestizo peoples. However, the value placed on Black or Indigenous was destroyed as a major effect of the slave society that emerged with the expansion of the sugar cane plantations. Family names, such as Mina, Carabalí, Congo, Angola, Lucumí, of our families and friends are eloquent testimonies to our African roots.

The central plaza and riverbanks were the domain of traditional White families. Right up to the beginning of the last century, some Black men and women still bore the imprints of slavery, branded skin, as was the case with animals meant for farm labor back then. Markers like "Arboleda," "Mosquera," and other family names could still be found burned in the skin of those who were barely beginning to forge a path for their freedom. At an intermediate distance from the town square were the Black families. As for the Indigenous people, they were nowhere to be seen in the town, except during market days. As I was growing up, I came to learn from family stories how tense the racial relations were and the differences between Mestizos and Blacks, Blacks and Whites, Blacks and Indigenous people, and so on, a chain of discrimination that made racial integration quite difficult.

Santander constitutes part of the subregion known as northern Cauca that, at the time of the formal abolition of slavery in 1851, had begun granting land titles to private individuals. In the wake of emancipation, many freed Black individuals were reluctant to return to work for the estates and former slaveholding families. Faced with a dwindling labor force, these families found themselves compelled to negotiate with the newly liberated people, conceding small plots of land in exchange for their labor in a process known as *terraje*. This arrangement was the only means to persuade the freed individuals to lend their services, as they had become more aware of the value of their labor and increasingly demanding regarding the fair distribution of profits. These men and women cultivated their land for agro-industrial development, establishing their own sources of income. This not only opened doors to educational opportunities and political empowerment but also laid the groundwork for social welfare for future generations. This process attracted many runaway slaves and recently freed individuals from other regions of Colombia to settle in northern Cauca—the land of my grandmother, my mother, my aunts, and myself.

Arriving in Santander, we would disembark from the bus just to realize that there was no transportation to take us home. We had to lift our suitcases and carry them across some seven blocks to our house. It was not until the nineties that the first taxis arrived in Santander. As such, to go to any part of the town center, you needed to walk for some ten to thirty minutes. Walking was a major piece of the people's social life, and at every corner, there was always some gossip or news that you were supposed to know. After my cousin and I had crossed several blocks, we arrived at our house. It was a house like any other in that region: a bungalow with a garden at the center and with a large courtyard, six sleeping rooms, having a kitchen and washing place at the back, with a large water tank in which I used to bathe myself with a gourd as a kid. Far behind the house was the yard, an empty piece of land planted with fruit-bearing trees and plantain shrubs and entwined branches, which we used as seating space, the perfect place for a family reunion during cool afternoons.

I remember the sound of the mangos falling on the roof at night. Every time one hit the metal roof, it reminded me I had to be the first to pick my share early the next morning. As a child, I was always afraid of climbing trees because of my lack of balance. So, whenever I wanted to eat mangoes, I either had to wake up very early to pick the fallen ones or beg one of my cousins to climb the trees and pluck them for me.

The regular entrance to the house was through the yard and the front door was always left open. When my cousins and I entered, everyone knew it was the family from Bogotá. Hardly had we set down our suitcases before the neighbors started shouting greetings at us from across the yard.

The yard was also used as a cooking space. That was where the soups and the sweets were made using the woodstove. It was also where we washed and combed our hair. As a child, I did not like combing my hair because I had the strange idea that it would make my head hurt and my hair would be pulled out. My cousins used to laugh at me for not taking care of my afro, for going around barefoot, and for not applying rubbing oil and always preferring to be free and without rules. However, when it came to tidying myself up at the end of the day and showing up as a well-kept, neat, and well-dressed girl, there was no tampering with the rules set by my aunt.

The simplicity of the place was quite delightful: to be able to enter any house, to walk around and have all within reach, to go to the waterfalls, to go fishing, and to sneak into the mountains of bricks and to swim in the public pool of the Quilichao river that was across town. Or just to walk from the plot close to the house to the river to watch the sunset and to witness the way women were busy doing laundry on the banks of the river. I very much enjoyed the ritual of the washing pool, how the women turned the river rocks into part of their ritual, and how each one of them showed off their dexterity in jerking their daily wear as their kids ran about the riverbanks.

Plans could be hatched at the spur of the moment; we only had to choose where to go. For instance, we used to go to the waterfalls known as the Indian cave or to a nearby river to catch fish. We used to prepare "white gold" (as we called rice) and a lemon and *panela* drink, knowing fully well that wherever we went, we would be able to cook, lay hands on some plantains, or meet some family member, however distant, who would supply us with chicken or anything else to put on our plate.

Every evening during the week, I would come out to sit with my aunt and my cousins on the sidewalk. I got to know the story of everyone that passed on the road, because as soon as we had exchanged "good evening" with the person and the latter moved a few yards away, family members would start sharing a detailed report on who it was, the name and the latest happenings in his/her life. I came to learn never to miss any of such moments, given that the person who had just stopped could turn out to be the main character of the family news agency.

During the day, we converted our block into a soccer field. We did not even require a proper ball—a plastic bag filled with papers was enough to set up the game. Weekend evenings were meant for feasting. People took out their speakers and sat outside to sing. On special occasions, they formed what was referred to as *verbena*: they would block the street and sing till daybreak. The popular music on such occasions was salsa and the ability to sing the latest songs was a cause for joy and happiness.

Chapter 6

The Strength of a Matriarchy

The ideas of territory, family, and community have been expansive in my life. For instance, my family circle is not limited only to my dad, my mother, and my siblings. My grandmother, my aunts, my fifteen cousins, and my close to twenty nephews and nieces constitute an inextricable part of my existence. My mother was a single mother and her relationship with my dad and his family was quite distant. I have been blessed with amazing female role models; I am the product of a matriarchy: my mother, my grandmother, my aunts, and my cousins.

My father and my mother were part of the colony of youths that migrated from northern Cauca to Bogotá in the early seventies in search of opportunities. They first met at one of my mother's friends' parties. Both forged a path in two public companies, the Bogotá Water Company and National Social Security Agency, enabling them to pay for their studies and obtain their professional qualifications, my dad as an accountant and my mother as lawyer. Their relationship was brief and not the best. I remember very little of my dad's visits to our house when I was a kid, and afterward I had a distant and sporadic acquaintance with one of his relatives when I was already an adolescent, as well as having lunch a few times close to his office. The truth is that a legal claim for child support against him was a turning point in my relationship with my father. Even if he provided some financial support, my contact with him and his influence or that of his family in my life were minimal. I have always sought to keep myself out of the tensions in my parents' relationship.

I spent the greater part of my childhood and my adolescent life in Bogotá, with my mother, my aunt Carmen, and my cousins Javier, Patricia, and Emelias. Without doubt, all the holidays spent with my aunt Cecilia and her kids in Santander de Quilichao were unforgettable moments.

CHAPTER 6

The women of my family had a great influence on my being. Engraved in my memory are the two women in Santander, my grandmother and my aunt Cecilia, who molded my character as a Black woman. Let me begin with my grandmother, who has remained a role model for me, a veritable symbol of liberty.

When I was appointed Minister of Culture, my grandmother's face was one of the first to come to mind. In her steadfast determination and tireless struggle, I saw the reflection of my own path. Whenever I was asked about her influence, I would explain, "My grandmother and my great-grandparents paved the way for me to occupy a space long denied to Black, Indigenous, and peasant people—a space in which we are still considered inferior beings." In these words, I tried to convey the weight of her legacy, the significance of her unsung work. For it was on the solid foundation of her life's work that I now stood, afforded opportunities that for more than a century had been inaccessible to people like us. Her vision, her tenacity, her indomitable spirit—these were the wellsprings from which I drew the resolve to soar, to shatter glass ceilings. With each mention of her name, I sought to pay homage not only to my grandmother but also to the multitudes whose stories, like hers, had long been overlooked. It was their collective struggle, their relentless work, that had made it possible for someone like me to claim a seat at the table of power that rightfully belonged to all, but was not for all.

María Remberta Zapata Guasá, my grandmother, was born on February 5, 1909, in San Rafael, a village in Santander de Quilichao. My great-grandparents were Gabriel Zapata and María Petrona Guasá Lucumí, both farmers among the first of a generation of African-descendant enslaved, with the challenging task of forging their own destiny and claiming their due rights of citizenship.

My grandmother, fondly called Berta, was the last and one of eight siblings, four of whom were women. She measured five feet, four inches tall, was slim, and had a short afro haircut. She used to dress in white blouses and mostly black or purple skirts that reached right below her knees. She was a woman of quick and determined steps. She had five children and raised as hers the child of one of her sisters who died during delivery. She never got married and used to work alone tirelessly to provide for her kids. She was both mother and father to them, given that she never had a permanent partner. She had a strong temper and was caring and generous toward her family members and her neighbors. There was always space and food in her house for everyone. She owned twelve pieces of land in two different municipalities in northern Cauca. As a peasant woman, she would sell her farm produce on Wednesdays and Thursdays at the Santander de Quilichao market square, and then on Sunday she would mount the horse to other markets in the neighboring municipalities. Her products included firewood, dragon tree leaves—used as sponges for cleaning plates—coffee, and cheese. During the rest of the week, she worked the farm, harvesting her produce and taking care of her kids and her home.

Berta lived in a mud house with a thatched roof and earthen floor, with three sleeping rooms, a parlor, and an attic floor accessed with the use of a bamboo ladder. Her home was surrounded by flowers and fruit trees. On her farm was heard the grunting of the pigs, the pecking of the fowls, and the mooing of the dairy cattle, not forgetting the neighing of the horse and the braying of the mule. She also had a well about twenty feet deep from which she drew water. The wood fireside was located outside the house and that is where she prepared her stew. She did everything by herself: from fetching firewood, slaughtering chickens, gathering the herbs to marinate it, cutting the plantain clusters, and making "the pot boil." In fact, there was no task at home that was above her.

She believed in God, and it shaped her daily routine. She rose at 4 a.m. every morning to pray the rosary devoutly, even when the roosters began to crow in the still dark hours. On Sundays, she walked two hours to attend Mass. Her unwavering faith was a family tradition—no one left the house without first receiving her blessing.

One of her main concerns was that all her children should be able to go to school, and she worked hard to ensure that they did. She always regretted that she had not been able to complete primary school. Despite her own lack of formal education, she was able to provide the necessary income to sponsor the schooling of her eldest children. The older siblings, in turn, ensured that their younger brothers and sisters received at least a basic education. It is through this family solidarity that my aunt Carmen was able to obtain a technical education and my mother a professional degree.

My grandmother was a woman of great determination and dignity. Even in the face of life's many difficulties, she emphasized that one could never afford to just sit and cry; rather, one had to keep going because even the most stubborn tears would eventually dry if one kept going. She often said, "Life is made up of both good and bad events, so we must be prepared for anything." In keeping with these philosophies, she constantly reminded us that we simply needed to move forward with our lives.

Berta passed away in Bogotá in 1980, shortly after my second birthday. She was seventy-one years old. In her final years, she had lived with us, her body paralyzed by thrombosis. During those afternoons, she would sit with me on her lap in a rocking chair by the window, holding and cuddling me with her strong, firm hands. The only words she could utter were to alert the family when I cried.

Perhaps that is why I feel so deeply connected to her memory—those days when her very breath of life seemed to pass onto me. I feel I knew her forever, her presence rooted in the core of my being. Even now, whenever I see an elderly resilient Black woman, I see my heroine: intelligent, capable, wise, energetic, brave, and a protective wall for her family. These are the women who, even in the darkest moments, beckoned us to see the glimmer of light in the firmament.

After my grandmother passed away, my aunt Cecilia, who I used to call Chila, became the head of our family, our matriarch. Chila was one of the greatest emotional cornerstones in my life. She was always there for me. I was her spoiled child, by virtue of being the youngest, the one who spent the entire holidays with her at the time when most of the kids had grown up and moved away from home. I spent every one of those days with her, glued to her side watching soap operas, walking slowly, and just contemplating her. I loved everything about her. A stoic and beautiful woman who, even at eighty—she took her last breath in 2010 in our hometown—did not have a single wrinkle on her face. She walked in slow steps and did not like exposing her body to the sun between eleven in the morning and four in the afternoon. She was the elder sister, the centerpiece of the family, one who would not get annoyed with anyone for more than five minutes, who knew about everyone's life even without asking them any questions. A woman who was widowed at a young age but who was, nevertheless, able to provide for all her nine kids who have grown to be very supportive toward each other.

Chila attended primary school in Santander but could not continue to secondary school, as it was reserved for men only at the time. So my grandmother sent her to the women's higher education center in the departmental capital of Popayán, known as "The Complementary." After returning to Santander, Chila met and married Juan at the age of nineteen. She dedicated herself to running the household. But when Juan died in 1981, Chila found herself thrust into the role of sole provider for the family, so she started a small home-based business making the sweet candy known as *manjar blanco* from milk and sugar. She also supplemented the business with farming, a skill she had learned from my grandmother.

Cecilia was a very simple lady, at once elegant and distant. She dressed in blouses and skirts that fell below her knees, always adorned with gold chains and earrings, not forgetting a ring that she wore all her life. She was always neatly styled, with thick frizzy hair that she used to style into braids twice a day. Whenever she appeared anywhere, people knew she was the lady of the house. She did not let anybody interfere with whatever she was cooking. Her daily ritual consisted in waking up in the morning and watering her plants, cleaning the leaves, and whispering to those heedful petals in a coded language that we never got to decipher: her garden was her confidant.

Aunt Cecilia did not often engage in overt discussions of identity or philosophize about such matters. Yet the essence of her being—her attitudes, her rituals, her haunting songs—indelibly bequeathed this profound legacy to each of us.

One song in particular, a traditional chant of the enslaved Black miners of the Pacific, would transfix us all whenever Cecilia sang it. With an emotional gravity that hushed the room, she would raise her voice to the chorus of "A la mina" (To the Mine). This resonated on multiple levels—as a reference to the family name "Mina" of her late husband, Don Juan, but also as an echo of the gold coast and slave port of Ghana, "El mina." When Cecilia sang this song, often while preparing lunch in the kitchen, a profound sense of nostalgia, justice, and a yearning for the future would fill the air. Her solemn demeanor made it clear this was no time for levity or interruption but rather a moment of reverent silence. It was as integral to her most intimate rituals as the tender care she lavished on her plants.

In the timeless lyrics, the weight of history and the indomitable spirit of the oppressed were distilled. Cecilia's quiet, resolute singing of this song became a living testament to the legacy of struggle and resilience that coursed through our family's veins.

In the evening, as we sat in the dining room, every so often one of my cousins would tell of how they were not allowed to get in this and that place in Cali for being Black. Before we started analyzing the situation and lamenting over it, Aunt Cecilia would gently but firmly bid us end the discussion. "Whatever people say or think about you," she would counsel, "should never cause you to divert your precious time and energy from doing what is important to you."

Her wisdom echoed in my own later years. As a minister in the government, I was besieged by a barrage of interrogations. It was during this challenging time that I remembered Cecilia's message of resolute focus. She was overjoyed to see me appointed and reassured me: "Everything will be alright. I will recite the rosary for you twice a day. You will always be my child, my Paula Marcela." She was one of the few to call me by my two names.

For me, Aunt Cecilia embodied a different form of power—a silent, molding force that shaped our very character, keeping us tethered to our hometown and family in a bond that endures to this day. Her measured words and unwavering equanimity in the face of adversity instilled in us a resilience and sense of purpose that transcended the obstacles society sought to place in our path.

The last time I saw Aunt Cecilia was on a rainy weeknight in Santander de Quilichao, where she lived with my cousins. I had just finished an event in Cali and, unannounced as was my preference, had persuaded a famous musician friend to accompany me on the visit. We arrived at Cecilia's modest home around 10 p.m., escorted by security.

As soon as she realized that I had brought a guest, she quickly went to her room to make herself presentable. When she returned, the five of us—my aunt, my cousins, my friend, and me—were sitting around the table. My cousin offered my friend a refreshment, and just as he took his first sip, my aunt asked, "Are you married, divorced, single, or what?" Caught off guard, my friend replied without hesitation, "All of the above." My aunt took a breath and said to me, "Paula, come with me to the room." I followed her to the room and confessed to her that he was just a good friend. She looked at me as if to say, "No, Paula." She was a very direct, affectionate, and protective person, always wanting to be in control of her territory. I offered her a gift I had brought for her, and she calmed down. But when we returned to the table, she offered my friend only a curt, "See you later" before retreating, nothing more. On our way back to Cali, my friend said to me, "For real, Paula, that aunt of yours is quite a strong woman." Yes, Aunt Cecilia was an amazing, unapologetically bold figure—caring, loving, and uncompromisingly clear in her convictions. In that final encounter, her fierce protectiveness and unwavering sense of family had been on full display, a testament to the indelible mark she had left on my life.

Chapter 7

Santander, Colombia, in Miniature

Santander de Quilichao greatly impacted the course of life in my childhood and my adolescent years. That town has always embodied something of a collective soul capable of expressing the complexities of our country, something between beauty and diversity but also a sense of permanent violence. Life and death co-exist with the same intensity, and the good is lived with the same level of extremity as the bad.

When I was approaching eight, circa 1985, I gradually became aware of the presence of the guerrillas. I was in Santander when the guerilla seized control of the town square. My cousins and I were playing in the swimming pool when, suddenly, one of my eldest cousins told us to immediately run to the house. "The boys," as the guerillas were commonly known, had just warned that they were entering the town. We wrapped ourselves in our towels, threw on our flip-flops, and ran to the house of one of our friends because there was no time to get to our house. The guerillas had passed an order that everyone should return home early and stay indoors. No one was supposed to be loitering outside when they entered with their trucks to rob the bank at the town square.

We hid in that house, all cramped in a single space, with lights switched off, panic-stricken, until we heard a loud alarm, a sign that the guerrillas had left and we were free to go out. We arrived at our house running, to meet our aunt who was waiting for us with anxiety. After that, we had to go to the house of the lone neighbor with a house phone in our block to wait for a call from my mother and my other aunt so as to let them know that we were safe. It was only close to midnight that we were able to visit the town square to listen to the rumors and witness the bullet marks on the walls of the bank that had just been robbed.

Santander considered itself a guerilla stronghold, and for many years it was assumed that they were good to the locality since they always warned us of their coming and had no other purpose than to rob the bank. However, as the guerrillas gained territory control and the scenario turned more complex, bombings, abductions, and extortion became part of daily life. The guerrillas became a real destabilizing factor for my family. Now it was not only about running for one's dear life out of the swimming pool but also from the house itself, that abode where I earlier believed nothing bad could ever happen to us. Afterward, I realized that, as a matter of fact, my childhood coincided with the highest presence of the guerilla in my hometown; that my adolescence would coincide with the height of drug trafficking and my youth with the era of the paramilitary, all in a row.

The 1970s marked the heyday of drug traffickers who could be seen patrolling the town square and the streets in very luxurious vehicles. They were called "magicians," given that the word "mafia" was linked to "magic," the magic of acquiring so much money overnight; seeing so many luxury cars and many other things that were new to us, as well as the degree of ostentation that characterized everything from sound systems booming all over the place and causing a huge fuss, to the jewelry. It was sad to see how young boys and girls who worked for them suddenly started showing off expensive brand shoes and other lavish products. These youths were referred to as *lavaperros* (dog washers), the private employees of the drug traffickers, charged with minor duties such as message carrying, monitoring, and driving, services that in effect constituted their initiation and their gradual promotion in the ranks of a criminal organization. Regarding drug trafficking, many families only noticed the consequences and many marveled in secret at the source of such enormous wealth, but everyone was careful and prudent enough not to dig too much into the matter. In my family, it was forbidden to talk about it; the less you knew, the better it was for you. Ask not and pry not too much—or not at all—was the unwritten rule that applied in the town when frequent assassinations and reprisals took place.

The most radical change in the life of the town was the advent of the paramilitaries in the late nineties. Suddenly, people started locking themselves indoors and protecting their doors and windows with wrought iron. Everyone covered their yards with canopies and closed off their plots. I recall one of my last holidays in the town at that time, the paramilitary order was for everyone to stay behind closed doors by eight o'clock every evening. Exactly at that time, they moved around in their trucks to see that the orders were followed to the letter. There was even a time when the families needed their authorization before organizing any kind of festivities. During those days, the conversations at home only centered on knowing whom of the town folks were to be called upon to provide the *vaccine*—as the paramilitaries referred to the parallel security tax, a euphemism for outright extortion. In those days, the atmosphere became very tense. Since it was no longer possible to step out of one's house without fear, we stopped spending holidays in Santander. I visited my aunt, but for short and sporadic visits. With time, the violence compelled many members of my family to live in different towns and to come to terms with the fact that the longed-for hometown had ceased to be the quiet and simple refuge it once was. The conflict completely altered the peaceful daily life of my childhood, especially in the last phase that saw a series of splinters among the actors: guerilla, drug trafficking, paramilitaries, and generalized criminality. A tiny Colombia, beautiful, fragmented, complex, and violent, that was Santander.

Part III

"A Black Woman ¿Born in Bogotá?"

Santander de Quilichao may be the place of my roots, but Bogotá—the great capital—is where I was born, grew up, and finally spread my wings. This modern metropolis of ten million souls is a study in contrasts, dividing its urban landscape along stark lines of social class. Wealthy northern neighborhoods gleam with the polish of a European capital, while the streets of the impoverished south and marginalized enclaves languish in poverty and displacement. Here in the heart of Colombia, the city prides itself on its elevated position—both literally, as an 8,000-foot savanna surrounded by towering mountain ranges, and figuratively, as the seat of national power. Yet this proximity to the sky only serves to distance Bogotá from the sea, enveloping it in a myopic insularity that stifles dialogue and fosters an ethos of individualism and indifference. It is in this complex, often frustrating crucible that I came of age, my identity as a Black woman forged by the shadows and glimmers of this city that I can never truly call my own.

I am a Bogotana through and through—in the way I speak, in the way I dress, in the way I perceive the world. Yet for most of my life, I have felt like an outsider in this city, a Black woman standing apart from the sea of Mestizo faces that surround me. It is an interesting fact that Indigenous, Whites, and Blacks are actually the minority in Bogotá, with a staggering 80 percent of the population identifying as Mestizo. But Mestizos often go to great lengths to deny their racial heritage, preferring instead to see themselves as White. Memories of my childhood days in Bogotá are limited to my neighborhood, the college, the homes of my mother's friends, and their workplaces.

I lived primarily in two neighborhoods that greatly impacted my childhood: Nueva Marsella and La Soledad. These neighborhoods were predominantly Mestizo, with my family always standing out as the only Black residents. In Nueva Marsella, we lived in my aunt Carmen Nidia's house, along with her three children. Nueva Marsella had the feeling of a close-knit barrio where everyone knew our names—the shopkeepers, the pharmacists, the neighbors. I spent lazy afternoons playing in these neighbors' homes or games of *la lleva* in the street. In la lleva, the thrill ignites when one player is randomly chosen as la lleva, the antagonist with the power to chase. This player sprints after the others, determined to tag someone. Once a player is touched, the pursuer declares, "la llevas," transferring the mantle of antagonist to their new target. The game unfolds in vibrant streets, where players seek hiding spots to evade capture, and laughter mingles with the exhilaration of the chase. With each tag, the excitement intensifies. This collective game fills me with a rush of adrenaline, serving as a metaphor for life itself—full of unexpected turns, heart-pounding moments, and the joy of being elusive in a world that often seeks to pin us down.

Our house in Nueva Marsella was a sprawling two-story affair, with six bedrooms, a huge kitchen, a living room, a studio, not one but two dining rooms, all surrounding a spacious patio, a two-car garage, and a front yard. It felt like we had so much space that we could easily accommodate fifty to a hundred people for the big parties on the first floor alone.

Then, when I was twelve, my mother and I moved to the La Soledad neighborhood. Here, our new home was only fifty square feet—more of a studio than a proper apartment. But it was ours, a modest first-floor unit with a small patio where we hung our laundry and tended a small garden. Though less grand than the house in Nueva Marsella, this apartment in La Soledad felt special. It was situated in an upper-middle-class area closer to downtown, near the green "Parkway" and the Bogotá River canal. My mother and I took pleasant daily walks to the nearby theater, stores, banks, and shopping mall, and it was also more conveniently located by bus to her office and my school.

What made this apartment so significant, beyond its cozy charm, was the sense of security and belonging it provided. It was our first place of our own, which my mother had made possible through loans and hard work, making the dream of a home for her and me a reality. We were always grateful for the continued support and community we found with my aunt Nidia and her family in Nueva Marsella, but this place felt like a new chapter for us.

In Nueva Marsella, I was fifteen minutes from my school. Since my classes ended at midday, I always had lunch at home. My mother worked full-time but never failed to prepare lunch for us, usually a meal of rice, grains, and some form of protein. After lunch, I spent close to two hours doing homework with my cousins because I was under their care. At four in the afternoon I eagerly watched my favorite soap opera, *Crazy Passion*, starring Carlos Vives, a great icon of Colombian music. It was about two young musicians fired up by the dream of success who ended up falling in love. After the soap opera, I remember that we had our daily chores, as my mother and my aunt kept a rotating list of tasks pinned to the fridge. At five o'clock in the afternoon, we were always in a rush since we had to finish everything between six thirty and seven in the evening, when my mother and my aunt came home, so that we could have dinner as a family and take stock of the day's activities. The two-hour long household chores were like a military routine, but they contributed greatly to our upbringing.

On Sundays, I would go with my Aunt Nidia to the marketplace. We would buy plantains, cheese, cassava, potatoes, some vegetables, and fruits (especially my aunt's favorites such as lulo, guava, banana, and passionfruit), and above all, fish and meat for the soup, which never failed to appear on the weekly menu. The saleswomen knew us so well that they often had our list ready even before we arrived. There were six or seven of us in the house, but we ate as though we were feeding twenty. Sunday lunch, served at three o'clock, became a cherished tradition, which created in us a very deep sense of family. We would all gather unfailingly and spend two hours sharing a special meal such as stew or some traditional dish. Afterward, we would tidy up and leave everything ready for the week.

By the time I was eleven, when I left primary school, I had learned to navigate the public bus system on my own. My mother had taught me how to take the various bus routes to get around the city, as my cousins had gone off to university and could no longer accompany me to and from school. Navigating the bus system was a whole experience in itself. The drivers seemed quite flexible, having to wait for passengers to board, stop on request, and even shout at people to hurry up. They would also have to jostle for space with other drivers, glance in the rearview mirror, and sometimes even flirt with attractive passengers. The drivers cranked up the radio, filling the air with their favorite tunes as they sang along. Meanwhile, they deftly ensured each fare-paying rider received the correct change. There was always a beautiful woman or a relative who did not pay the fare who was invited to bypass the register and sit close to them. I often wondered how they managed to juggle it all at once. This chaotic yet lively system allowed me to navigate the city with a sense of independence and adventure.

By managing the transport system, I was able to participate in a variety of afternoon and weekend activities, including volunteer groups. In 1992, I joined the Youth Center, a Catholic youth organization, which marked a pivotal point in my life. The Leadership Schools run by the Youth Center gathered young leaders from churches or schools to embark on an experience of defining their life's purpose, their call to service, and to work on their spirituality through activities like reading the Bible, praying, physical exercise, connecting with nature, and learning to live and work with others. On average, there were forty to fifty leaders from all over the country and sometimes from other Latin American countries like Venezuela or Puerto Rico. Over the years, I took on various leadership roles, eventually becoming a director of these Leadership Schools.

I spent most of my weekends at the headquarters of the Youth Center, known as La Capilla. Located two hours from Bogotá, La Capilla was originally an old hotel that had been gifted to the organization's founding priest by wealthy families. To reach this site, one had to walk down a stony road through bamboo groves and towering trees covered in moss and lichen. The temperate climate and lush natural surroundings fostered a sense of intimacy, as morning fog and dew gave way to warm sunshine, inviting exploration of the twenty-house compound and the adjacent crystalline river that meandered through the property. The gentle sound of the flowing water created an atmosphere of tranquility and peace. It was in this serene setting that I connected with my inner self, listening to the soothing rhythms of the river, praying, reading, and practicing meditation by the lakeside. In the evenings, the group would gather around campfires, with someone strumming the guitar, sparking my deep appreciation for the idealistic music of Silvio Rodríguez, Pablo Milanés, and Mercedes Sosa. It was during this time at La Capilla that I experienced a profound spiritual and political awakening, further reinforcing my sense of purpose.

After completing high school, I decided to take a year to work with the Youth Center, delaying my university studies—a decision that my parents did not initially support. I had passed the entrance exams to study psychology at the university, greatly influenced by my cousin Patricia, who was already a psychology student and had introduced me to the works of Freud as a child. However, during that year of working in different municipalities and churches and building leadership experiences for hundreds of school students every day, I realized that psychology was not my true calling. More than just analyzing and understanding human behavior, I wanted to build structures and set up teams aimed at producing measurable results. It is for this reason that after finishing my year as a volunteer missionary with the Youth Center, I settled on pursuing a degree in industrial engineering instead.

The hands-on work I had done with the Youth Center, organizing leadership programs and witnessing the tangible impact they had on young people, had shown me that I wanted a career path that would allow me to create sustainable solutions to societal challenges. This change in my academic direction, from psychology to industrial engineering, was a pivotal moment for me. It marked the beginning of a new chapter in which I would put my experience at the Youth Center to use addressing complex social issues. The solid foundation I had gained through the Leadership Schools and my time at La Capilla headquarters had cultivated a deep sense of purpose and passion for using my skills to make a tangible difference in the world.

From the very first semester, I knew I had found my field. Industrial engineering focused on producing goods and services, making it possible for me to understand the way systems and processes function. However, halfway into the first semester I felt the need for more studies in the humanities, so I decided to study Italian language and culture.

My interest in the cultural legacy of Italy began way back, when, as a teenager, my mother gave me a birthday trip to the Island of San Andrés, the place of the seven-color sea in the Colombian Caribbean. It is a paradise of music, such as reggae and calypso. There, I was transported to a different Colombia, one where creole came before Spanish. A black Island with beautiful Baptist church structures made of wood. In the hotel where we stayed, I met an Italian man who completely fascinated me: a tall man with hazel eyes, brown hair, straight and plentiful, with a perfect smile, and who wore a red silk scarf, approached me and told me his name was Giuseppe. I told him my name only in return, unable to communicate with him because of the language barrier, and I resolved that I would one day learn Italian. That is to say that it was platonic love that motivated my initial desire to learn Italian.

While at university, I also decided to step back from the Youth Center. I wanted to explore other forms of social work beyond the religious focus of the organization. This is how I gained inroads into academic spaces that were more centered on political training and community engagement. I became closely involved with Javeriana University, where I took part in a seminar on Colombian affairs and contributed to the creation of a volunteer group working with a sugarcane-producing community located about an hour from Bogotá. This community had been hit by a natural disaster, and our task was to apply our technical know-how and resources to help the community recover and rebuild.

My mother started getting used to having a daughter who was always on the move, engaged in three to four tasks at the same time, and who woke up very early and returned home late. This situation only became more difficult as I further immersed myself in my work with development agencies, universities, and social movements—often spending considerable time abroad wherever my efforts were needed.

The shift away from the Youth Center toward academic and community-based initiatives marked a significant evolution in my approach to social work. While the Youth Center had provided a solid foundation in spiritual and leadership development, I now sought to apply those skills in contexts that addressed systemic socioeconomic challenges. My time at Javeriana University and my work with a rural community allowed me to see firsthand how I could leverage my technical expertise and social-work skills for collaborative problem-solving, driving meaningful, community-led change.

This transition was not always easy for my family to accept, as my schedule became increasingly demanding, and my focus expanded beyond the religious sphere. However, it was a necessary step in my personal and professional journey, one that would ultimately shape my career path toward becoming an agent of social and political transformation.

Chapter 8

A Communist in the Family

My aunt Carmen Nidia was a towering, influential presence in my life, embodying a paternal role that had a profound impact on me. With my father absent from my daily life, she stepped in as a formidable authority figure, offering guidance and, at times, gentle correction. Her unwavering support and wisdom filled the void, shaping my values and helping me navigate the complexities of growing up. She dedicated her time to nurturing my dreams, actively engaging in designing strategies to help me achieve them. Carmen Nidia was a tall, slim woman with an imposing afro or braids. She was the first woman in the family to wear short skirts and high heels in the sixties, embodying a revolutionary spirit. She was the politician, the yogi, the world traveler—venturing from Russia to Venezuela and Cuba. She was always committed to multiple causes, from positive thinking clubs to founding rehabilitation centers. In all senses, she was progressively minded, far ahead of her time.

Carmen Nidia's passion for social justice and progressive ideals had been cultivated from a young age, shaping the remarkable trajectory of her own life and career. She studied business and graduated in 1960, at the age of seventeen. Thanks to her training, she secured a job with the trade union of a sugar-producing factory in Palmira, a medium-sized city close to Cali. She was the first in my family to venture to work away from Santander de Quilichao. Carmen Nidia then moved to Bogotá, as part of a generation of Afro-Colombians arriving in the capital in search of opportunities. There, she got a job with the Avianca Workers' Trade Union, making Bogotá her home for nearly half of her life. Bogotá always confronted her with the unwelcoming attitude of the capital toward Blacks and people from other regions. She told us how shocked she was to notice that people scratched their knees each time they saw a Black person, as a sign of good luck. She and her friends were determined not to be limited only to jobs related to domestic service and manual labor. They studied at the technical and professional levels in Bogotá and almost all of them ended up working in various state institutions. It was during the 1970s that Carmen Nidia left Bogotá, by then already married, to live in Barranquilla. While there, she continued her work with various trade unions in the metallurgical industry. It was in Barranquilla that she became a member of the Communist Party, even being proposed as a candidate for the City Council, though she did not win. Political affairs, however, remained a central part of her life. A few years later, she returned to Bogotá and rejoined the Avianca Workers' Trade Union, where she worked until her retirement.

My aunt spoke little about her political militancy, even though we knew it was always bubbling within her. In fact, her first trip abroad was to Moscow, and no one in the family knew about her plans. At that time these things were kept under the rug. She was one of the founding mothers of the Union of Women Democrats, the women's wing of the Communist Party, eventually becoming its president. Every year she took us along to the march for workers' rights on May 1. The music played in our house often included workers' movement anthems; I particularly remember one about the Spanish Civil War, with the title, *Que culpa tiene el tomate* (What Guilt Has the Tomato Got). Aunt Carmen's convictions had an impact on certain decisions we took in our lives. One of my cousins decided to study in Czechoslovakia, and Aunt Carmen wanted her daughter Patricia and me to be integral parts of her experiences and efforts, trying to mold the next generation of women in the family. Once a month, it was a ritual for us to have lunch in her office and discuss my life plans. It was during these sessions that we agreed my first foreign trip alone would be to Cuba when I turned fifteen. In each meeting, she schooled me on a specific theme, like how to save money and organize myself to achieve my goals. As well as some piece of advice that has remained close to my heart, for example: "Paula, always remember that in whatever you do, the most dedicated person earns what is hidden. You earn everyone's will." She was a high-energy, open-minded woman, determined to live life fully and face its challenges head-on.

One of the most defining moments for us all was when leaders of the Patriotic Union, a movement to which she belonged, became the subjects of targeted killings. The Patriotic Union was a leftist party created in 1985, bringing together the Communist Party and members of the former guerilla groups as a result of a political process of reintegrating the latter into civil life, thereby granting them the opportunity for political participation. In just over two decades, more than two thousand members of the Patriotic Union were assassinated or "disappeared" while many others received death threats and were forced into exile. My mother remembers having seen Aunt Carmen in tears after the assassinations of two presidential candidates, Jaime Pardo Leal and Bernardo Jaramillo, and the leader Manuel Cepeda, all of whom were her close friends. And I well recall how on each occasion she was dressed elegantly with a deep aura of sadness for the funerals of her fallen comrades.

These deaths weighed heavily on her, leading her to reconsider her political involvement. The final straw came when the army raided our home. Someone had tipped off the police that we were harboring suspicious people, possibly even hiding weapons, because of my aunt's militancy. When I was around nine, the army stormed our house one night and ordered all of us to the parlor, where we were surrounded by more than thirty soldiers. There we stood, in our pajamas, as they searched through the house, rifling through wardrobes, looking under the beds, and checking every other space they suspected might serve as a hiding place, even the ceilings and the bathrooms. The next morning, my mother, who shared many of my aunt's ideals despite never being a militant herself, advised her to reconsider her affiliation with the Patriotic Union. Our home was now on the radar of military and intelligence forces, and political leaders and activists were being threatened and killed—this was a clear sign of the great risks we faced. In light of these frightening incidents and given that in her fifty years she was now on the verge of retiring from her job, she chose to step away from political advocacy and dedicate herself exclusively to social causes.

Carmen Nidia died on June 14, 2000, at the age of fifty-seven, from a devastating stomach cancer. I had just returned home after spending some time in Switzerland. My return marked the beginning of her decline, and, to a great extent, the beginning of her farewell. Every time I met her, it was clear to me that she was approaching the end but that she still had several projects she hoped to see through. I remember one day I was at the university and they called for me because they wanted to take my aunt once more to the clinic, but she was unwilling to leave the house. I tried to talk her into going. I entered the room, closed the door, and began to talk to her face to face. "We have to go, Aunt Carmen. Tell me what causes you pain or what's troubling you." I helped her off the bed and settled her on a chair right close to the window. She sat there for a few minutes and the sadness in her eyes left me with the premonition that she was not going to come back alive. Again, I asked her what was worrying her, and she started calling out the names of her children. Finally, she turned around, looked at me, and said, "I have finished the race. May we meet again." I sat there looking at her and then took her hand with the infinite affection I always felt for her. I did not ask her anything else. In silence, I waited for her for a moment and said, "Aunt, we have to go now." She stood up, refusing my support. That was her last burst of energy in her house. Standing at last, she was visibly weak and finally let us hold her: she asked to walk slowly through her house, room by room, staring into space. Amid the silence, each step and moment looked like a rehearsed farewell. God alone knows what she was saying to each of these spaces. The truth is, she never returned.

In her final moments, she confided to us that she wanted a mirror placed on her coffin, so anyone curious enough to see her face for the last time would instead see their own reflection. Right to her very last breath, she remained a special woman. Carmen Nidia's worries, aspirations, and revolutions have always lived on, and shall forever live, within me.

Chapter 9

Bogotá Flares Up

By the time I finished high school and started university, Bogotá had become the flashpoint of violence at the national level. That which during holiday in Santander de Quilichao had appeared to me as something sporadic, now turned into a permanent sensation in the capital city.

The late eighties and early nineties were dramatic years. I still have a series of hazy images and sensations, trying to understand what actually occurred. I felt like the country was going through a baptism of fire with tragedies that were no longer isolated cases but part of an intimate daily reality. You could sense the restlessness in the air, from the seizure of the Justie Palace by the guerrillas, within a few blocks from my mother's jobsite, to the explosion of car bombs that rocked the streets and, on several occasions, could be heard right from our home. The news on the air was, the Minister of Justice, four presidential candidates (Luis Carlos Galán, Bernardo Jaramillo, Carlos Pizarro, and Jaime Pardo Leal), and the director of one of the major newspapers of the country, *El Espectador*, have been killed; a bomb had exploded at the Embassy of the United States of America; in the Administrative Department of Security; in a plane, in a pub, in a mall; they have attacked, seized, detonated, and so on and so forth. All these military terminologies became buzzwords. I recall the days of the curfew or the days when activities were canceled, when people had to remain indoors due to the funerals and the explosions. The order was that everyone should stay at home for the country was going through critical times. Even though my mother and my aunt were not all that worried and granted us much liberty, they cautioned us to spend as much time at home as possible, for anything was possible anywhere. The general atmosphere in the city and the entire country became very tense. The drug cartels and their leaders were gaining more and more attention.

Drug trafficking, terrorist attacks, army, paramilitary, guerilla, exiled, threatened, extradited, kidnapped, cartels, capos, arms caches, and other similar terminologies started flooding into our daily language. It was a challenging and disconcerting time for everyone.

With the passage of time, the massive insecurity of those days thawed for a while, and in the early years of the new century, we felt at home in our streets once more. Not that the conflict had ended once and for all—the flashpoint simply moved away from the major cities. The phenomenon of violence took other forms in more remote parts of the country where massacres, armed strikes, and invisible boundaries started emerging, accompanied by news of military operations and demobilizations. In this atmosphere, in a universe full of complexity, I kept growing and coming to terms with the fact that this was, and is, my country. Over the decades, the situation has improved, but many security challenges still linger.

Part IV

The Horizon of My Dreams

As soon as the morning light broke, my mother, María Zenyde Zapata, would turn on the radio to fill our home with her favorite salsa melodies. This ritual became my first memory, the soundtrack to my life even before I took my first breath. My mother is a natural artist, and her gift lies in the way music uplifts her spirit. The melodies she embraces are not just notes, they also are declarations, while the lyrics resonate deep within, transforming her every movement into an expression of feeling that adds flavor to our lives.

She embodies music as much as she embodies dance. Whether it is a subtle nod or a full-bodied sway, rhythm is her constant companion. When a truly great song plays, the volume rises, and we all join her in celebration, especially on weekends when we have the freedom to let loose. From my earliest memories, she would coax me to dance, urging me, "Lift up those feet of yours . . . move your body." Through her, I discovered my love for music and dance, a bond that transcends generations. In those moments, we would be transported to Santander de Quilichao, a place where music wove our family together. All it took was a good speaker to ignite an endless party, whether in the living room or on the streets. Music became our daily ritual, a lifeline that kept us connected to our roots. While my way of speaking, dressing, and social etiquette reflect my Bogotá upbringing, my choice of music and my dance moves—those are gifts from my mother, deeply rooted in the vibrant culture of Santander.

María Zenyde is the youngest of her siblings, a vibrant blend of temperament, practicality, and humor. In 1968, at the age of twenty, she moved to Bogotá, where she pursued training as a medical assistant in a dental clinic. This foundation enabled her to support herself as she later fulfilled her dream of becoming a lawyer at the age of forty. My mother was truly a woman ahead of her time, choosing to embrace single motherhood in an era when it was far from easy. Yet she approached every challenge with immense pride and determination, always focused on the future.

I vividly remember a moment at school when a boy asked, "If Paula has kids with a white person, what would they look like? Like cows, with black and white patches?" Another child even touched my arm to see if I would lose color. Confused, I turned to my mother, asking if it was abnormal for a White person to have children with a Black person and why people thought our skin could discolor. She simply replied, "Paula, I am pretty sure your young friend is the product of a White person and an Indigenous person, or he may have a Black grandfather. Did he come out with patches? It is just a matter of ignorance. Case closed." Rather than delving into what other people said, as did Aunt Cecilia, she preferred to focus on stressing our humanity, possibilities, and aspirations.

My mother instilled in me the habit of thanking God for our abundant daily blessings, emphasizing that true wealth lies not just in material possessions but in the time we spend together, caring for one another. When I was twelve, I remember accompanying her to a rehabilitation center in a neighborhood known as "Cartucho." At first, I wondered why she would not let me stay home and watch TV instead. There, we encountered the stark realities of drug addiction; many shared how they had believed they could control their use only to become ensnared in a web of dependency. I witnessed both the relapses and the remarkable strength of those who fought to reclaim their lives. This experience taught me a profound lesson: that every decision, no matter how trivial it seems, can have lasting consequences.

She has been a philanthropist without realizing it, often involving me in her charitable activities—supporting rehabilitation centers, organizing medical clinics in vulnerable neighborhoods, and hosting Christmas celebrations to provide gifts for children of low-income families. I witnessed her and my aunt Carmen share whatever we had with those in need, and it can be no coincidence that I would later go on to establish a foundation. I gradually became the realization of the dream they nurtured in me every day. Since then, my mother has opened her home and heart to many leaders I have asked her to support in my absence, creating a network of adopted children who, alongside me, care for her and consider her both a mother and a friend. In this way, although we lost a significant part of our family, my mother forged new connections and new families. To this day, she sends messages of love and encouragement to those dear to her, wishing us beautiful days and showering us with blessings.

My mother found unique ways to shape my character; I remember a pivotal moment when I was twelve. I had gone to the bathroom to try a cigarette, but my mother quickly caught the scent of tobacco. Instead of scolding me, she took out a pack of cigarettes, showed me how to inhale deeply, and then made me smoke the entire pack, one cigarette after another. Dizziness overtook me, my eyes watered, and I felt nauseated. Once I was sick, she calmly said, "If you want to do it, you must see it through to the end." From that day on, I developed a strong aversion to smoking, a lesson learned through her unconventional parenting methods.

Her usual response whenever I proposed something was always the same: "Why not?" From a young age, my mother instilled in me the belief that nothing was off-limits for us, encouraging me to chase my dreams and desires—provided they were legal, ethical, and caused no harm to others. She often urged me, "Today, today, today, Paula," reminding me to embrace the present fully, just as she does, turning every moment into a celebration. She also taught me the value of saving, giving me a piggy bank each year while maintaining her own, which only accepted five hundred– and one thousand–peso coins. Those coins were sacred, while she tucked away bills in books or notebooks, always reminding me that one never knows when they might be needed.

"Listen to your smile," she says, her eyes sparkling with sincerity. "I do not like people who do not smile, Paula. A smile is the universe's strength." Through her, I learned the importance of smiling at life, embracing its challenges, and continuing forward with hope and determination.

After retiring at fifty, my mother dedicated herself to exploring the world mainly through a group called The Friendship Force, visiting more than forty countries. From the majestic ruins of Petra in Jordan, to Lisbon—her personal favorite—to the pink-sand beaches of New Zealand, she seized every opportunity life presented, often borrowing against her means without a shred of regret. Whether riding a camel, floating in a hot air balloon, embarking on a safari, or cruising along the Nile, she resolved to pursue her adventurous vocation after fifty, repeating frequently to me,

"I won't leave you an inheritance; rather than accumulate wealth, I will spend every last bit of my resources living life to the fullest."

I vividly recall her recounting a trip to Greece, her voice filled with wonder as she said, "My mother couldn't afford to buy the history book for school, and I remember gazing longingly at a picture of the Acropolis in a classmate's book. When I finally stood before it in Athens in 2009, I felt incredibly blessed. Who would have imagined that, back then, when we could not even afford a book, I would one day see that monument up close?" My mother, who had previously traveled only to neighboring countries—Venezuela for goods to sell, Ecuador with the family by car, Panama, and Cuba, our family's obligatory destination—was now exploring every continent. Her home became a gallery of her adventures, adorned with plates that marked the horizon of her dreams and achievements. She began gifting these plates to those she loved, a living legacy of her journey.

It is no coincidence that I have become a nomad throughout my life, even though my home and roots are always in Colombia. From an early age, my mother entrusted me with her wings, only to reclaim them when she sensed my own were beginning to unfurl. Her journeys opened the world to her, illuminating the path for my own adventures and reminding me that horizons are boundless. Together, we learned to fly—she soaring with renewed spirit, and I ever inspired by her fearless embrace of life.

Yet, for her, it was not easy to have a nomadic daughter, often absent and consumed by work as I traveled the globe. Our relationship became strained during my time as a minister; we grew distant for months, and eventually, she stopped speaking to me for over a year. It was not until I returned from my scholarship in the United States that we began to mend our bond. We are like water, air, and fire—two emotional, strong-willed, and fiercely independent women. When I moved into my own apartment, stepping away from being the center of her life, it became a grieving process for her. However, in that space, she learned to rediscover herself, realizing that the true center of her life and the foundation of her existence was, and always had been, herself.

In 2014, my mother made a bold decision to sell her apartment in Bogota, calling me not to consult but simply to inform me of the date I should come to say goodbye. When I asked her why and when she was leaving, she replied with determination, "I have decided this is what is best for me at this phase of my life. I am going, even if I do not have a place to call home yet. I will stay with your cousins for a few weeks and begin a new life, Paula. You will have your other home in Cali."

The moving truck rumbled down the streets of Bogotá, its cargo a lifetime of memories packed into boxes, while the storage unit stood as a silent witness to the transition. Everything was already in motion, propelling my mother toward Cali—a vibrant city just forty-five minutes from Santander, a ten-hour drive or a half-hour flight from the capital. But Cali was not just a destination, it also was a promise of warmth and color. With temperatures consistently hovering between 77- and 85-degrees Fahrenheit, it offered a lush landscape, alive with parks and greenery, a stark contrast to the often gray and distant Bogotá. Home to two million inhabitants, Cali is a city alive with a rich tapestry of culture and diversity. Nearly 30 percent of its population identifies as Black, infusing the city with a vibrant spirit and a warmth that makes it particularly welcoming to newcomers. This multicultural blend not only shapes the community but also enriches the local traditions, creating an atmosphere where music, dance, and celebration thrive. In Cali, every street corner seems to pulse with life, inviting you to experience its rhythms and flavors. Known as the salsa capital of the world, Cali promised my mother the joy of weekly dance nights, where she could lose herself in the rhythm and connection of family and friends. Here, life moved at a slower pace, imbued with flavor and warmth, a refreshing departure from the cold confines of Bogotá. In Cali, she envisioned a new chapter, one filled with laughter, music, and a sense of belonging.

Days later, I found myself landing in Cali, stepping into the role of my mother's caretaker as she sought a new place to live. Each apartment I liked was met with her disapproval, until eventually, she discovered a charming residential complex where retired teachers gathered. At sixty-five, she was ready to start her new life. In this vibrant community, she blossomed. Every day, she made her way to the pool for hydrotherapy, engaging in an hour of dynamic exercise followed by half an hour of spirited gossip with her neighbors. She cooked alongside them, took leisurely walks, and immersed herself in five different dance groups. Moreover, she organized philanthropic efforts, ensuring that children in the most vulnerable neighborhoods of Buenaventura and Cali experienced the joy of Christmas. This marked a new beginning—an opportunity for a vibrant and peaceful chapter in her life, as she reshaped her existence and drew closer to our larger family once more.

Maria Zenyde embodies strength and resilience. We have faced the heart-wrenching task of burying half the family we once knew, yet she has held onto her yearnings, memories, and nostalgia without succumbing to the weight of the past. Instead, she has drawn us all—my cousins' children, her nephews, and me—into her warm embrace, becoming the last living link to her siblings and a sanctuary for those who remain. A friend for life, my mother has always been ready to share any experience I propose. She embodies sharp honesty, grounded in profound wisdom. Over the years, she has learned to express her truths with increasing candor and prudence. My mother has consistently lifted me up, and through her, I have learned to navigate the complexities of life with courage.

Chapter 10

Other Worlds

In 1994, having turned sixteen and prior to the one year I spent at the service of the Youth Center, I received my first gift for completing high school: a trip to Cuba. The trip was the brainchild and the making of my mother and my aunt who decided that since my cousin Patricia had made the same trip after finishing high school, it would be fitting for me to follow in her footsteps. I spent two weeks traveling on this island that fascinated me with its sense of Caribbean spontaneity, full of music and coquetry. It was my first time traveling alone, and from the moment I arrived in Havana, I felt so much at home.

I visited numerous villages, drank countless mojitos, and found myself endlessly humming the song that would become one of my favorites, "Lágrimas Negras" (Black Tears). Until this day, my Cuban friends keep asking me what I like in this song. They even go to the extent of telling me, "Paula, this song is that of a jilted and drunk dude." But I love it, nevertheless.

Some words of José Martí have remained engraved in my mind. A Cuban writer, poet, and revolutionary thinker, Martí is renowned for his passionate advocacy for Cuban independence from Spanish rule and for the abolition of slavery. Born in 1853, he became a pivotal figure in Latin American literature and politics, blending his literary talent with a deep commitment to social justice. One quote in particular has resonated with me since the first day I read it in the plaza of Santiago de Cuba: "Palenque, a divided people is a dead people."

In Cuba, I began to ask questions about political issues. Though I didn't fully grasp the complexities at the time, I was struggling with the quest for equality and the uneven distribution of resources, all while navigating a landscape of limited freedom. I encountered sharply divided opinions:

some believed fervently in the revolution, while others felt imprisoned by a complex regime.

I romanticized Cuba as an idyllic place. Nonetheless, I was also aware of this other side of the Cuban reality that I did not want to judge, but which revealed the loopholes and the contradictions. I was very touched by the African influence in Cuban society, be it in the music or the dance, but even more: as a Black woman, I also felt the weight of race. I started noticing the profound racism in daily life. Once a police officer climbed on a city tour bus and started yelling *jinetera*, slang used for sex workers. As I fumbled for my passport, the police officer came close to me and was almost about to drag me out by the arm. It was only the intervention of the tourist guide and fellow passengers that prevented him from succeeding. They explained to him that I was a young Black Colombian woman, not a prostitute, and that they had not hidden me in the bus nor was I there for any service of any kind. Often, I was the only one stopped by security as we entered the hotel. To be a Black woman in Cuba, dressed like a tourist, in shorts, sandals, and shirt, or in whichever attire, singled you out as a prostitute. It was the very first time that, out of Colombia, I felt the weight of race. The moment they mistook me for a prostitute spurred me to think more deeply about the value of one's body, the fact of being a woman, and society's perception of pleasure.

Despite the difficulties, I fell in love with Cuba. But more than the enjoyment of travel, I realized that exploring other worlds wasn't just about having fun. More than that, traveling allowed me to step back, immerse myself in different cultures. It made it possible for me to explore and to recognize myself and to be the Paula that I wanted to be in spaces where no one knew who I was.

Between the ages of eighteen and twenty-two, I lived in three different foreign countries: first in Italy, then in England, and finally in Switzerland. I left to study in Italy in 1997. I spent months exploring various cities and small villages, feeling the magic—what Italians call *il fascino*—of a country whose historical weight filled me to the brim. Every day, I would walk around for hours, led by my travel guides in Milan, Florence, Rome, Venice, and Siena, among other places. I visited museums, churches, historical ruins, and of course, the *trattorias*. I fell in love with Italy, not just because of the handsome guy I had met in my teens but also for the fact that the baker, the gateman and any passerby would greet me with, "Ciao bella." I thought it was because they found me stunning. "What a marvelous country!" I thought, only to realize later that it was just a common greeting to any female passerby.

In the summer of 1997 I started studies at the University for Foreigners of Perugia. It was right at the time of the jazz festival, a great distraction but I enjoyed every bit. During the week I would study, and in the evenings I attended cultural events. On weekends, I traveled by train to nearby villages in the Umbria region. The festival rekindled the same sense of Africanness that I had felt in Cuba. One day, I moved from watching a metal band from New Orleans to witnessing a ballet from Guinea whose movements resembled those of *mapalé* and other dance styles from the Colombian Caribbean. I felt so moved that I cried. A Colombian friend who had come to visit me looked at me, astonished, and the only thing I could say to her was, "We are the same." I really cannot explain what I felt at that moment. It was like looking in the mirror and discovering a part of myself that I had never before been aware of. That once far-away Africa was standing right in front of me, telling me, "You too are part of me."

Italy greatly shaped my sensibility and my taste for art. I fell in love with Dante's *Amor ch'a nullo amato amar perdona* and the poet Giacomo Leopardi's cantos that echo it; with the architecture; the emotion triggered in me by the *Duomo* of Milan—a majestic Gothic cathedral—and the Basilica of St. Paul Outside the Walls in Rome, with its splendid mosaics. The first time I visited Spoleto's Bridge of Towers—a magnificent bridge of ten arches in the middle of a valley that connects two mountains with a precious waterfall on one of the sides—made me think about the aesthetic vision of olden day structures. The bridge only served as a connecting point and an aqueduct, but it also provided a panoramic, bird's eye view of the entire Umbria region.

I was captivated by the paintings of Leonardo da Vinci. I could spend hours upon hours just staring at them, allowing myself to be absorbed by the expressive force of human nature and the enchantment it transmitted with its multiple forms, depicting human day-to-day realities, attitudes, and contradictions. For me, Italy also came to stand for surrealist cinema: Nanni Moretti's *Palombella rossa* became one of my favorite films. The movie begins with a car accident; suddenly, an adult man is standing in the swimming pool, about to dive into the water, in a line with five little kids. He stands there, pondering aloud whether he should or should not jump, going through past scenes from his life and trying to answer the question, "Ti ricordi?" (Do you remember?). An incredibly beautiful experience, about what we choose to remember and why, in the same way that sometimes our memories and our excessive reason block us, preventing us from behaving like little children and from taking the risk to live in the moment before everything comes to a stop. Italian cultural expressions have always made a great impression on me.

On my way back to Colombia, I spent three days in London. I was instantly drawn to the city. Walking along Oxford Street and Piccadilly Circus, I felt like I was at the center of the world. I was moved by the diversity of the people I saw in the streets. "I really want to study here. I like this country, I like this city." At that time, I did not speak English and felt I could not fully enjoy the beauty of the place without knowledge of its language. So I called the British Council Office in London and obtained the phone number and the address of its Director for Latin America, Peter Sandiford. I sent him a letter and he introduced me to the Director of the British Council in Bogotá, John Bryant. John scheduled an appointment, and I talked to him about my desire to learn English, to pursue my postgraduate studies in England by getting a scholarship. I insisted and succeeded in convincing him. It was then that he offered me a scholarship for off-peak hours (with fewer students during the day) on condition that, if my performance was satisfactory, the scholarship would be extended. I promised to go in for the highest level. And that was it: in twelve months, I had reached the advanced level thanks to the fact that I had pleaded with a friend who had once lived in the United States to teach me and lend me her English course books. Another reason was that I had asked my cousins to give me their music CDs in English. I studied English on my own every day from four to six in the morning.

"Are you leaving us again?" That was the question on everyone's lips in the family when I celebrated my twentieth birthday. I had completed my degree in Italian and had an advanced level in English, even though I knew I still needed to polish my English proficiency. So I started looking for a scholarship to study in England. I sent more than fifty application letters to various English language institutes in England asking for scholarships. After a few months, one of them yielded fruit and the director of a Brighton-based institute called and offered me a scholarship for the following summer.

My aunt and my mother provided the ticket and gave me some extra money. I left for Brighton to live with an English family and to study with a group of Italian, Swiss, and Japanese friends. I enjoyed not only the pubs and the discos of Brighton but also the natural environment of its beaches. The peculiarity of those beaches was that they were not of sand but rather of small pebbles or "shingle" and even in the heart of summer, the water was freezing. During weekends, I enjoyed hiking along the Brighton cliffs, which I found utterly delightful.

After completing my course in Brighton, I spent a few months in London, where I was welcomed by a friend who also hailed from Santander de Quilichao. I enjoyed spending the end of summer in London, where I had the opportunity to explore and visit my favorite museums several times. I succeeded in getting a job selling ice cream during the day on Edgware Road, just a stone's throw from Oxford Street. It was an interesting job: the little kids smiled at me while the adults tried to make eyes at me. In any case, I found the overall attitude of the people very nice.

England represented a harmonious blend of the past and the modern. Every now and then I listened to the song "What Could Be Better?" by an English band called Lighthouse Family. It was my everyday morning hymn to express my gratitude for the gift of life, existence, and opportunities. In fact, what could be better than starting to discover the world, and not just England but also soon the possibility of visiting Switzerland?

During my time in Brighton I had already begun looking for an internship because I wanted to stay longer in Europe. I applied to twenty internships that I had found on the internet. Out of the twenty, I received two offers, one in Brussels and the second in Geneva. I opted for Switzerland, to work with the United Nations Conference on Trade and Development (UNCTAD). One of the factors that motivated my choice was that a friend of a friend from my Youth Center days lived in Switzerland and could help me get settled into life there. I counted myself lucky that among the eighty thousand applicants from all over the world, I was chosen, and I ended up as the only intern from all of Latin America. That is how I moved from London to Geneva.

CHAPTER 10

I was seduced by Geneva. I loved walking its streets, and in the late afternoon, I enjoyed strolling on the banks of Lake Leman, with its backdrop of snow-capped mountains and the imposing figure of Mont Blanc in contrast. At night, I would go for a glass of mulled wine at the historical city center and just while away time by walking around and enjoying the place. Apart from my colleagues at the United Nations, my circle of friends included the artists living in *squats*. They became my informal French teachers. Just as my wish to learn Italian was inspired by a teenage crush, my motivation to learn French came from Julien Amy, a classmate from Brighton. He was a tall guy with small black eyes, thick eyebrows, and a beard packed with gray hair. Along with his short hair and cream-colored skin, it seemed to me a perfectly attractive combination. During the farewell ceremony of our language course, his gift to me was Charles Baudelaire's poem "À une passante." The poem was carefully wrapped in a purple ribbon, written on a blue-colored handmade sheet, in delicate and impeccable italics, with an ink that invested it with an extra romantic charge. I still have it, even today. The poem recalls a magic moment, perhaps such as the time Julien and I first met, a moment in which seemingly nothing serious happened even though there was always this sensation that something could have happened had we dared beyond a certain threshold.

When I started my internship at the United Nations in Geneva, it felt to me like the entire world had been reduced to a single spot. I followed and analyzed the positions of the country representatives of the different member nations and appreciated their distinctive stances. Trying to comprehend the context and the way they built consensus was a great learning process for me. That said, I was really struck by the overwhelming bureaucracy and began questioning the meaning of it all. After weeks of hearing mostly rhetoric, I found myself growing bored. In many plenaries, I wondered whether the representatives of developing countries were engaged in a merely cathartic exercise or whether their voices were heeded at all. It often seemed like that their counterparts from the so-called developed countries often left immediately after delivering their own speeches. Still, I reminded myself that, as an apprentice, I had to keep my questions to myself and focus on absorbing everything I could from the experience.

At first, I struggled with the impersonal atmosphere of the offices, especially with tacit rules such as not to interrupt your colleague during office hours and eating alone at one's desk during break. So, in my office, and those next door, I instigated a more personal rapport given the diverse cultural composition of our team: two of us were from Colombia, two from Africa, one from the Netherlands, and the other from Italy. We initiated coffee breaks and a small get-together on Friday afternoons. That is how I made many friends and celebrated my twenty-first birthday in style, in the presence of the entire team and the director of our unit. The latter never missed a chance to remind me that I was "too young to be here."

I had my very first boss at UNCTAD, a marvelous German lady named Katja Weigl, who told me she had selected me because she was putting together the World Foreign Investment Directory and needed someone fluent in Italian. She was of average height, with fair skin, a slim build, blond hair, and light-blue eyes that hid under her trademark spectacles. Though her voice and her manners were gentle, her arguments were sharp and strong. Katja was a structured, systematic, and rigorous type who wasted no time. She always had everything thoroughly set before our meetings, whereby she would not only correct the nature of the contents but also the double spaces that I had the habit of leaving between words. Her professionalism and her spirit of excellence greatly marked the level of commitment to duty that I have always strived to demonstrate in my own professional life.

Switzerland was unique for the job and the friends but also for the fact that I could make the best out of its lakeside cities. I enjoyed the mountains and the French, German, and Italian cantons, three cultures that lived together with a degree of order and harmony that was astonishing to me. I felt like I was in a place where everything was programed and controlled. Switzerland was magical, yet a bit distant and cold. It was beautiful and glamorous, but it always gave me the sense that I was just passing through.

Chapter 11

Only for the Children of Presidents?

I returned to Colombia in the year 2000. I had two specific objectives in mind: to graduate as quickly as possible and to find a master's scholarship opportunity abroad. My work at the UN had ignited a deep passion for development issues and international affairs, and through conversations with my colleagues, I discovered that everyone was pursuing either a master's or a doctorate. The competition was fierce, and I knew I needed to stand out.

When I landed in Colombia, it was crystal clear that I had to get a postgraduate degree from a prestigious university to open doors globally. In 2001 I graduated with a first degree in Industrial Engineering, and in 2002 I did some consulting work, but it was not easy to find a permanent job. The head of the department at the Autonomous University offered me some short-term jobs, and my cousin's friends also gave me some ad hoc jobs, but I struggled to find the steady employment I craved.

Before completing my undergraduate program, I had meticulously researched master's programs that aligned with my aspirations. Cambridge University stood out, with two compelling options: a master's in Community Development and an MPhil in Management Studies. I was admitted to both, but ultimately chose the MPhil because I felt it offered a broader spectrum to explore my interests with a stronger emphasis on research.

When I shared my intention to study at Cambridge, a family member dismissively remarked, "But Cambridge is only for the children of presidents." At that moment, I felt a surge of determination. This was my dream, and I was going to make it happen. Over the next two years, I devoted myself to the arduous process of securing funding, even though I lacked the level of experience required by scholarship bodies in Colombia.

At the international level, I was shortlisted for a scholarship but didn't make it to the final list. Undeterred, I kept on trying, even going so far as to request the support of the university from which I had graduated and the one where I wanted to study. I also competed for a Credit-Scholarship scheme. In 2003, these three attempts finally paid off, and I sought to convince my long-time mentor, Yezid Viveros, and my mother to sign the promissory note and place their houses on mortgage for me. The debt I contracted was huge, given the very high living and study costs in England. But the most important thing was that I was able to fulfill my dream of returning to England in 2003 to study at one of the best universities in the world, which I had barely heard of during my brief passage through London on my way back from Italy in 1997. My family organized two great parties for me with all my friends in attendance: a farewell ceremony featuring marimba and chirimía music by a group from the Pacific whose members were friends of mine, and a more intimate gathering with only family members. That one of us could study at such a renowned university seemed like a miracle and an immense source of pride for everyone.

I arrived in Cambridge in September at the beginning of the fall. The beginning of my studies in Cambridge constituted a significant shift in my approach to learning. Whereas my previous educational experience had largely involved the teacher providing comprehensive explanations, the Cambridge method emphasized questioning and independent inquiry. Rather than passively absorbing information, I was challenged to actively engage with the material, conducting individual readings and analyses to develop my own understanding. The role of the professor evolved, shifting from lecturer to facilitator—providing examples, guiding discussions, and probing my conclusions to ensure I truly grasped the course content. This dynamic learning environment ultimately fostered a vibrant network of academic connections, and as a student I learned to present my ideas in a manner consistent with the principles of inquiry, honing my ability to construct well-reasoned arguments. This skill proved invaluable when communicating with my diverse classmates, representing more than twenty different countries and backgrounds, as well as when engaging with distinguished guests such as Nobel Prize winners, industry leaders, and global policymakers. Through this process, I refined my ability to express myself clearly and confidently, framing my ideas and questions in a structured, thoughtful manner within an atmosphere of mutual respect and open-mindedness.

The most important person to me during my time at Cambridge was my academic supervisor, Peter Nolan. A tall, slim English professor with long, frizzy gray hair, he had a peculiar habit—he rarely stood still while lecturing, as if his ideas flowed more freely as he moved from one corner of the room to the other. Occasionally, he would stop suddenly, his entire body beginning to shake as he reached the climax of the argument he was developing, his hands dramatically outstretched. Peter had dedicated his life to the study of China and its development model. In my interactions with him, he played a crucial role in shaping my professional and personal aspirations as a development practitioner and instilled in me a strong capacity for action-oriented analysis. Our early meetings, however, were quite challenging. I had to prepare meticulously by reading at least ten books and countless articles, synthesizing and elaborating my ideas, and presenting my conclusions. For the first four meetings, however, Peter simply dismissed my arguments and instructed me to return only when I had something truly useful to contribute rather than merely regurgitating what I had read.

Peter's relentless push for deeper critical thinking forced me to spend more time in the library, to ponder ideas while walking, bathing, or sitting alone in a cafe. Gradually, through this process of trial and error, I began to structure my focus, until finally, during our fifth session, Peter declared, "You have begun to think." From that point on, our meetings grew in length, from a few minutes to a half hour or even an hour, as Peter introduced me to a network of academics and experts. I always remember his advice during our final session: "Paula, do not focus all your attention on the score and the assessment. No doubt, you are going to pass. But what is certain is that people won't value what you write the same way you expect. But let that not discourage you, Paula. Let me tell you that what you are thinking and how you are arriving at it is what matters. The true test of knowledge will be life itself. Concentrate your efforts in preparing yourself for it." His words, echoing within me, have shaped the very trajectory of the self-confidence of my path forward.

My master's program was research based, and I chose to delve deeply into the development models of local communities, primarily Afro-Colombian and Indigenous populations, along Colombia's Pacific Coast—one of the world's top ten biodiversity hotspots. This study addressed critical issues surrounding the African diaspora and the complex interplay between development and the environment. I was driven to unravel one of the greatest paradoxes of Colombian reality—that the resource-rich Pacific region was also home to the country's highest levels of poverty. I approached this research with a keen awareness that the true measure of my work would be its ability to illuminate meaningful insights and inspire real change. As I delved into the complex dynamics of the Colombian Pacific, I sought solutions to the striking disparity between natural wealth and human impoverishment. I knew that this research would serve as a critical foundation for the path ahead and shape my contribution to the field of development.

Colombia was at the very center of my time in Cambridge, and I had the immense privilege of founding the Society of Colombians alongside thirty of my compatriots. It proved a profound educational experience, as we invited experts to analyze the complexities of our nation's history and conflict. Undaunted by the deep-seated ignorance surrounding Colombia, we organized a series of lectures and photographic exhibitions that shed light on the multifaceted realities of our homeland. After these events, I would often hear remarks from friends of other nationalities that betrayed their profound misunderstandings. "Hey, Paula, so there are tall buildings in Colombia? I could hardly believe it—I thought it was just a country where everyone ran around in the forest being chased by guerrillas!" Indeed, the extent of such misconceptions continues to amaze me to this day. For many, it seemed simply inconceivable that a country so wracked by contradictions could still progress economically and socially rather than stagnating in the quagmire of conflict. Yet the most joyous moments always came after the formal proceedings had ended—when each of us would bring a taste of home, be it a beloved Colombian dish or a refreshing drink, to share in celebratory gatherings at the homes of our fellow members. In those moments, we were not merely Colombians, but Colombians to the very core of our being.

CHAPTER 11

I made the most of my Cambridge experience from day one. So much so that my friends teased me on graduation day, joking that my active social life and extensive travel had effectively earned me degrees in management, public relations, and tourism. I will always remember the first letter I received from my mother the following November, at the beginning of winter, in which she said, "Paula, know that everyone holds the key to their own happiness. It does not depend on others. You have the choice in every situation. If you want to be happy, cultivate this inner disposition, make the best of every situation and do what fulfills you."

Heeding my mother's advice, I immersed myself wholeheartedly in the vibrant social and cultural scene that Cambridge had to offer. While I pursued my studies diligently, I also made sure to take full advantage of the university town's diverse range of activities and communities. In the evenings, I made sure to organize a dinner with my friends from the same dormitory. Together we formed a small Tower of Babel—three Indians, a Chinese student, a German, an Austrian, and me. This international student exchange allowed us to develop unique codes of conviviality, blending elements of Colombian hugging traditions, Indian curry cooking, and German-Austrian beer culture. We eagerly shared pieces of our respective backgrounds and broadened each other's horizons.

After dinner, I often found myself drawn to the pulsating rhythms of different musical worlds. On Tuesdays and Fridays, I would lose myself in the vibrant salsa scene, my body swaying to the infectious melodies that filled the air at PoNoNa Bar, and then Café Africa was my connection to the vast universe of African music. But it was on Wednesdays that I truly felt a sense of liberation as our tight-knit hip-hop group descended into the magical, subterranean realm of the Fez Club. This basement venue was a veritable oasis, a wonderfully streetwise space that stood in stark contrast to the academic confines of my everyday life. The atmosphere was electric, pulsing with the vibrant energy of the locals who frequented this underground sanctuary. It was here that I truly fell under the spell of hip-hop, the rhythmic incantations of the DJs weaving a spell that resonated deep within my soul. I will never forget the moment I first heard the opening bars of my favorite Notorious B.I.G. track, "Big Poppa," and instantly felt the music pulse through me. The infectious chorus echoed in the air, urging me to dance until dawn. My New York classmates became my guides in the art of hip-hop, teaching me not just the moves but the rhythm of life itself. In that vibrant underground space, I shed the weight of my academic persona and embraced the raw, unfiltered essence of my true self, losing myself in the beat and the energy that surrounded me.

And on weekends, I took advantage of the low-cost airlines to visit several European countries—France, Luxembourg, Holland, Belgium, and even Italy again. I was determined to make the most of my time abroad, immersing myself in the vibrant social fabric of Cambridge while also exploring the wider continent.

The lectures, my academic supervisor, my college mentor, my housemates, my party friends, and the Colombian students were all central to that transformative year in Cambridge. However, another profoundly awakening experience for me was the Professional Development Program offered by the university. This program confirmed what I had intuited during my time at the United Nations: that the sky was truly my limit. Emboldened, I began applying for positions with humanitarian development agencies in countries facing escalating conflicts, such as Sudan. But when I was finally shortlisted for one of these coveted positions, a difficult decision had to be made. My mother's impassioned pleas convinced me to return home, arguing that there was so much vital social work to be done in Colombia and that we had a debt to pay. Torn between my global ambitions and my filial duty, I found myself at a crossroads—one that would forever shape the trajectory of my life's journey.

In late 2004, at the age of twenty-four, I returned home to Colombia, bidding a farewell to the hallowed halls of Cambridge. My first job upon my return was as a research assistant in the Faculty of Administration at the prestigious Universidad de los Andes. There, I immersed myself in the analysis of foreign environmental policies, under the tutelage of the former minister of the environment Manuel Rodríguez. This entry into the world of academia was made possible by the recommendation of Professor Malcolm Deas, whom I had met during my time as President of the Colombian Association in Cambridge. Our warm relationship had blossomed into a genuine friendship, and it was this bond that compelled him to open doors for me back home. Deas was an old friend of Manuel Rodríguez, and he had made this opportunity possible for me. However, I did not rely solely on this connection—I also actively knocked on many doors on my own. I sought out contacts at USAID and the US Embassy in Colombia and was excited to learn that they offered opportunities for young Afro-Colombians. I contacted the director of USAID at the time, Michael Deal, and asked to be considered, which paid off as he submitted my resume to several operators and provided me with invaluable contacts. Within a few months, I had secured a position as a consultant and began managing international cooperation projects in programs in the Pacific region and among Afro-Colombian communities.

At the same time, I forged a close working relationship with two officials at the US Embassy in Bogotá—Milton Druker, the Deputy-Head of Mission, and Anne Callaghan, the Director of Public Affairs. Together, we established a program that would enable young Afro-Colombians to learn English, apply for study scholarships abroad, and undergo leadership training. Both Milton and Anne understood the importance of inclusion for ethnic minorities, not merely as a professional commitment but also as a matter of deep personal conviction. Milton was an average height, White, and slim man with broad spectacles that concealed a rather noble, deep, and astute gaze. Anne, on the other hand, was a tall slim blond with light eyes and short hair, a woman of undeniably caring character. Both became my trusted allies; they believed in me and gave me unwavering support. In fact, when Milton, then acting ambassador, got wind of the possibility of my appointment, he personally assured the president that he knew me well and that I had the full support of the US government.

I shared with Milton and Anne how language skills had opened doors for me, and we formed a working group in order to advance the Afro-Colombian agenda. Once a month, we would meet to follow up on our initiatives and discuss next steps. They used to frequent places close to my office, and so we invented two traditions: going to eat hamburgers or visiting the only Jamaican restaurant in the entire city, given that Milton had fond memories of his time as a Peace Corps volunteer in Kingston. Our collaborative efforts culminated in the establishment of the Martin Luther King scholarship program in 2004, which enabled more than a thousand Afro-Colombian and Indigenous youths to learn English and pursue advanced degrees at some of the world's finest universities. Today, over two decades, many of these scholarship recipients occupy positions of power in sectors that were once foreclosed to us. For these young people, the exceptional was not a matter of innate talent but rather access to transformative opportunities.

Amid the whirlwind of new professional opportunities, teaching remained a constant source of joy and fulfillment. The opportunity to lead impactful development projects proved to be the perfect complement to this passion. Ultimately, I returned to Colombia with a renewed sense of purpose, determined to forge a path that would uplift my community and leave an indelible mark on my country. This was just the beginning of an exciting new chapter, one in which I would use my skills and connections to drive meaningful change.

Chapter 12

The Other Colombia

My job in international development cooperation took me to the Pacific region of Colombia, a place often referred to as "the other Colombia"—an epitome of backwardness, isolation, poverty, and above all, of all that which is Indigenous and Black, not fully recognized as an integral part of the country. Despite coming from a Black family with very little racial mixing, from a locality just a few hours from the Pacific coast, I knew little of that region. The only thing I recalled was the talk in our family meetings about the marked difference between Blacks from the interior (us) and those from the coast (the others). Visiting and getting to know the Pacific region presented an opportunity to learn about the nuances of my identity as a young Black woman. After all, the majority of the country's Black population is concentrated along the coasts, particularly in places like Palenque, Chocó, and the Pacific. Each journey to these areas became a personal awakening, a chance to understand more deeply the dimensions of my racial identity as Afro-Colombian—something that in Bogotá I could not fully see and understand.

In late 2004, I found myself in Quibdó, the capital of Chocó on Colombia's northern Pacific coast. Though the flight took less than an hour, arriving felt like stepping into a foreign country. Just mentioning this part of the country as my destination sparked surprise and curiosity. I later learned that it took more than ten hours by car to traverse the 105-mile road linking Medellín to Chocó. The road, a perpetually unfinished government project, epitomized the persistent neglect of these communities, not just marginalized but seemingly forgotten by the country itself. I ventured into the Chocó that was largely unknown to most people, yet it was recognized internationally as a biodiversity hotspot—one of the thirty-four regions in the world with the greatest diversity of species and ecosystems. This unique environment, with its significant ecological advantages, became the focus of my research in England. Despite studying its megadiversity, I realized how little I truly knew it. Hidden in the heart of the humid tropical forest, Chocó was depicted in books as a refuge for enslaved Africans seeking freedom—a territory viewed as distant and savage, valued only for its natural minerals and timber resources. Media narratives cast Chocó as a Colombian version of Africa, but not the Africa celebrated as the cradle of humanity. Rather it was a stigmatized version of Africa shackled by backwardness, exploitation, and colonialism for which no one takes full responsibility. This created a simplistic perception of Africa with a static history, stripped of any future prospects.

As the plane touched down in the rain, I gazed at the landscape below—a dense forest stretching like an endless olive-green carpet. From the window, I could spot a horde of small, scattered settlements, more like an ensemble of wooden houses with a church at the center and all nestled along the banks of the expansive and imposing Atrato River. Quibdó, the region's capital and a city of more than one hundred thousand inhabitants, had the same appearance. It looked like a patchwork of the settlements that I had seen from above, its infrastructure pieced together in a seemingly chaotic sprawl. The landing strip was so short it made me think that we might take off again due to lack of space to slow down. As the plane's door opened, the humid air hit me with a sudden intensity, soaking my skin in a mixture of sweat and moisture. It was another world that, although unknown to me, I could not explain why it nevertheless felt familiar and near.

The streets were worn and filled with potholes. Some of them were unpaved and were littered with trash. At first glance, I was left with the impression of a disorderly and neglected city. But once I entered the homes and the buildings, the warmth of the people—expressed by their hands, their smiles, and their welcoming words—conveyed a sense of mental order and dignity.

The community councils constitute the organizational schemes for collective property among the Black communities in Colombia. Jointly with the Indigenous reserves, they own eighty percent of the territory of the Pacific coast. In one of my first meetings with the community councils of the Atrato River (Cocomacia), one of its leaders told me, "We want to dialogue with you, but without impositions. . . . Remember that we are equals and no one masters our territory and our process better than we do." Their message was clear: they were the primary agents of change, and any collaboration would have to be built on mutual respect and understanding of their history and struggle. I was touched by their sense of self-pride, that of a people who continued to fight for its structural freedom.

In Quibdó, there was no public transport system, so I quickly became accustomed to hopping on a motorcycle to get around—a situation that remains unchanged today. I took delight in climbing onto the bike; the fresh breeze on my face offered a welcome reprieve from the heat, even though the bumpy streets made speeding impossible. These rides allowed me to gossip with the motorcyclists about food, politics, and rumba at every corner. Through them, I stayed connected to the pulse of the city. I loved the vibrant spirit of its people and cherished the warm exchanges, like the women greeting each other loudly with "Ave, manita" (Hello, my sister), filled with affection and generosity. The men and women walked as if they were dancing through the streets. Walking was not merely about reaching a destination quickly; it was a form of art that expressed style, taste, and a deep sense of Black identity. Amid the disorganized yet charming architecture, observing the people passing by was a captivating sight.

The rain was a blessing from the sky. It allowed families to collect enough water in anticipation of inevitable dry spells. At the time, nearly every household had tanks for capturing rainwater. (Piped water arrived only years later and still serves only a small portion of the population, primarily in the town center.) Since it rained very often, most women moved through the streets with their colorful umbrellas and their shower cap on their head. They rarely removed them, fully aware that at any moment the rain—ever their faithful companion—could return. Moreover, the rain exemplified a profound attitude toward life—an embrace of patience and acceptance in the face of oblivion, much like the steady fall of raindrops to leave things to come to pass, to let life take its course. It was a surrender to nature, a reminder to let life unfold at its own pace, even amid uncertainty. In this way, the rain was not merely a weather pattern, it also was a philosophy, echoing the rhythm of this vibrant community I had come to love.

In the afternoons, I often walked along the breakwater, and once again there was water, this time in the form of a large river, the Rio Atrato (Atrato River), the fastest flowing river in the country. Its name is believed to reference the slave trade—el Río de la Trata—a poignant reminder of history. I could witness the boats coming and going—long wooden vessels laden with the day's cargo, covered in thick black or green plastic. When lifted, these tarps unveiled hordes of red lulos, vibrant orange-red fruits that resemble small, fuzzy-skinned tomatoes, their bright green interiors filled with tiny, edible seeds. Alongside them were peach palm nuts and clusters of green bananas, creating a colorful array of tropical bounty.

The engine boats were often piloted by tall, confident Black men whose dexterity was evident in the way they navigated the rushing river with calm authority. Their steady gazes were fixed on the horizon, as if to assert their mastery over the waters. In contrast, small boats navigated by Black and Indigenous women glided through the water with a different grace. With modesty and skill, they balanced their boxes and bags, leaning onto poles for stability while deftly pushing their paddles. I lingered at the breakwater, mesmerized by the scene unfolding before me. As the sun dipped low, the sky ignited in shades of orange, casting reflections on the water and blending the deep greens of the forest with the warm rays of the horizon. The wooden houses on the opposite shore began to glow with light, creating a harmonious chorus of illumination. In that Chocó, I not only found a new sense of freedom but also began to grasp the true meaning of family—one that intertwined with the rhythms of both nature and community.

Amid this vibrant scene at the river, I couldn't help but reflect on the deeper currents running through Quibdó's history. Until the 1960s, the city was marked by overt racial segregation that permeated its spatial, educational, and economic life. A devastating fire in 1966 swept through the commercial center, prompting many White and Mestizo traders to flee, while the Black majority remained. They took control of the city, starting to cope with the contradictions of self-governance and isolation by the central government. The city and the state had long been plagued by corrupt and mediocre leadership, a situation that shook me to my core. I will never forget meeting one of its governors. The meeting took place in a riverside building so decrepit it seemed ready to collapse. Everything around us felt precarious and battered. At the end of the table sat the governor in a white sleeveless undershirt, a towel draped over his shoulders to wipe the sweat from his brow. His casual posture suggested he was in his living room, starkly contrasting the dignity I had observed in the head offices of social movements and community organizations. He greeted us and lamented, "It is very difficult for anything to happen or change here. It's a tough place." I felt a wave of indignation wash over me. How could the highest authority in the region utter such defeatist words? I took a deep breath, grappling with the stark contrast between the dire needs of the people and the presence of someone who seemed to believe we were wasting our time. After a heavy sigh, he added, "The truth is, no one bothers about this place—not even its leadership . . . honestly, it doesn't bother us, and that's why it is this way." I couldn't help but wonder how the people could choose such a leader—someone who, without hesitation, exhibited a devastating lack of governance and vision for the future. Chocó had never seen a governor capable of taming its tumultuous history, one that had kept an entire population stagnant. Instead, its people bore the burden of electing individuals who, even as sons of the soil, sought power solely for personal gain, failing to achieve even the most basic necessities for the community.

It was within that dense, vast, and impenetrable forest of Chocó that an important component of my dreams began to take shape. Echoing the sentiments of Gabriel García Márquez in his memoir *Live to Tell the Tale*, I found myself discovering "a totally unthought-of country within our country, of which we were completely unaware." Chocó revealed itself as a magical realm of vibrant forests and eternal downpours, where reality often felt like a far-fetched version of everyday life. Amid its contradictions, Chocó offered invaluable lessons to the nation about alternative forms of development, autonomy, and beauty. Amid the neglect, it remained a land of possibility. Ultimately, what emerged from this experience was not merely the other Colombia, but rather the other Paula—a new version of myself.

Chapter 13

The Other Paula

As my travels along the Pacific coast continued, I found myself not only visiting Quibdó once a month but also immersing myself in the vibrant streets of Buenaventura and Tumaco, two major capitals of the region. My time was split between holding talks and designing projects with community leaders from women's and youth associations, community councils, and churches, while simultaneously battling the internal struggles within the cooperation agency where I worked to prompt timely decisions. The latter proved far more challenging.

I had built strong relationships with the communities and grasped their urgent needs, especially in the face of rising criminality. This "other Colombia" had embraced me as one of their own, and I felt a deep responsibility not to let them down. As internal conflicts within the agency intensified, I reached my limit. After ensuring that all requirements were met and cooperation agreements signed, I decided to resign from my position as project manager for Chocó and coordinator of Afro-Colombian affairs. My resignation was deeply personal, and it stirred discomfort within the organization; I began to appear more as an activist than a project manager. I found myself at odds with the organization's values. They seemed more concerned with pleasing the priorities of Bogotá's elite nonprofit organizations—those who wanted to "save Chocó" without ever having set foot there—than with supporting the courageous grassroots efforts of the communities in urgent need of resources. Once the necessary funding was secured, I made my decision to leave.

A week after my resignation, I received an unexpected call from two leaders of the Community Councils of Guapi and Timbiquí, with whom I had previously met in Bogotá. These towns, smaller than Quibdó, Buenaventura, or Tumaco, each boast an average population of around thirty thousand, seventy percent of whom live in rural areas. They were named after the rivers at their banks. The leaders expressed that as soon as they learned of my resignation, they believed I was the right person to serve as a project advisor for their regional ethno-development plan. What moved me most was their determination to gather resources to cover my honoraria and travel expenses, despite their own limited means. I knew little about these territories, but their willingness to make such a sacrifice deeply touched me and affirmed the trust they had placed in me. Without hesitation, I accepted their offer, and the following week, I was on my way.

In preparing for my trip to Guapi and Timbiquí, I asked about the possibility of road transport, only to learn that even today, no proper roads connect these towns. The only way in was by air or sea. After about half an hour in a small plane that shook like a leaf in the wind, I landed in Guapi. This time neither the heat nor the humidity surprised me; my body had adapted to the Pacific climate, though I still found myself sweating.

In late 2006, at the age of twenty-six, Guapi struck me as distinctly different from the other places I had visited—not only in size but also in its pristine, natural beauty. Upon arriving at the airport, which was little more than a large open-air hall, I hoped to find a car waiting to take me into town. Instead, I was greeted by a group of community leaders ready to walk with me down the unpaved street to the town center, a journey of about fifteen minutes. In reality, the "center" was the entire locality, as both Guapi and Timbiquí stretched along single, populated roads. We headed straight to the wharf, the true gateway to the town. Flanked by water and lush forest, it also served as a playground for children who took turns diving into the water, competing to see who could make the most skillful splash.

I had never navigated the rivers of the rural Pacific before. I arrived, unaware, as an uptown girl, with a flashy suitcase and high heels, completely out of sync with the reality and the lifestyle of these places. My first pitfall was when I clumsily boarded the boat at the wharf. Only then did I realize that I had assumed most of Colombia was like Bogotá. My pride as a girl from the capital city blinded me to the context of these communities, about which I had no previous knowledge and where sophistication lay in other aspects of life, such as being able to draw blue crabs from a basket halfway through our boat trip when we felt hungry.

My second misstep came when I asked everyone to look after my suitcase so that it would not fall into the water, for the fear of losing my clothes. The locals looked at me, wondering why I was so worried. It was as if they were making fun of me, and their astonished eyes conveyed something like "this child is going to come out of this trip a totally changed person." We went downstream until we reached the sea. In the middle of the trip, I noticed the narrow nature of the estuaries in contrast to the immensity of the sea, where one gradually learned the way the water conversed with the forest while the sea waves reflected the change in landscape. In that region, water acted like a mirror and its sound had something intrinsically musical about it.

We stopped at the house of the Torres family, the music dynasty of Guapi. They were a group of men with a sly, deep, and keen gaze with broad smiles that shone against the backdrop of their Black skin. Each sound of the drum and every touch of the marimba with the strength of their Black, peasant, and robust hands transmitted an ancestral force of freedom instilled by the rain, forest, sea, the movement of the trees, which emerges from the dark and fuses with daylight. These marimbas, made from beach palms, are an adaptation of the African xylophone that survived and thrived despite all the attempts by the slave society to crush its expression. I just thought: such a cultural miracle! Music was a major means of reconnecting with the distant African home and constituted the collective will to re-create in the middle of banishment. That was the significance of the house of Torres, an open hall with marimbas of different sizes hanging from the walls. The sound produced by these large forest pianos echoed like water entering the body through the ears, with the tenderness and the force of the forest, a cheerful lament of an Africanness re-created in the quest for freedom. It was my first time witnessing a live marimba ensemble in its natural space; the magic of this ancestral instrument resonated deeply in me.

We continued our way. I was fascinated by the olive-green color of the water that contrasted with the beauty of the mangroves and the forest. We passed through the estuaries and gradually entered the sea. I was deeply impressed by the immensity of the scenery and could only say to myself, "What a privilege!" "What a paradise I'm in!" We entered back into the river to reach Timbiquí, and it took us some time before we got to the town, specifically to the house where I would stay. It was already dark. When I got off the boat my shoes were soaked in water. Everyone looked at me with a sense of indulgence, expecting me to remove my shoes and assume my true self in my new abode that was ready to receive me with open arms. There was no electricity in the locality, no way to charge my phone or computer. This was a bit stifling, but at the same time, it enabled me to commune more with nature and with the locals. Life was more genuine in that way.

The following morning I awoke to a chorus of forest sounds. I could not say for sure which sound was from which animal. Not all were from birds or frogs. There was much more, but I was unable to make them out given that my affinity with animals had always been very basic and pitted with deep fear. Even though the toilet was nothing more than a latrine, I thought there would be the possibility of a proper bath. But when I saw my five companions come out in their shorts, undershirts, and with soap in their hands about to go down the stream to bathe, I came to the reality. They only said to me, "Paula, aren't you coming with us?" My only worry was that I had not brought my swimwear. If I decided to wear another piece of clothing, who or what was going to watch me? As all this was going through my mind, they were already relishing the effect of soap lather on their bodies as they bathed in the stream. Without hesitation, I put on my shorts and undershirt and followed suit into the river. In the end, I happened to be the one who was reluctant to leave. I waved at those passing in their boats and just abandoned myself to the flow of the environment. The following days I got to know a group of kids with whom I would go out to bathe in the stream and have fun in the afternoons; meanwhile in the mornings I relished the possibility of bathing happily and nearly bare-bodied with the grandmothers. As a matter of fact, no one was watching me; I was another member of the community.

Being without a refrigerator and any groceries, I naturally worried about what I would eat, aside from the crabs. However, for the lady of the house, food seemed to be the last thing on her mind. She only had to ask someone close to her to "go and cut down some plantains," while another person should "light the wood fireside and bring a pot of water," and a third should go get three of the fishes caught the previous day. The woman would gather some herbs from the terrace, grown in small quantities on a wooden tray hanging from the roof. This simple setup was common in the area, as the herbs were used both as spices and for first-aid treatments, acting as the community's basic pharmacy. With just a handful of herbs, plantains, and fish in the pot, the secret to the first meal of the day was born. Mornings featured different types of fish, seafood was served during the day, and in the evening, you could enjoy a light fish soup or a delicious plate of yuyo, a risotto made with nettles.

This was true life. At various times in the day, people would gather to take a sip of tomaseca, a distilled drink that was stored underground, mixed with medicinal herbs to enhance its fermentation and was consumed by women as medicine for fertility and an aphrodisiac. About half an hour after drinking it, I always felt the urge to take a nap because it made me feel unusually cheerful and caused me to sweat. Gradually, I realized that most of the things that seemed so important to city dwellers, or in most of the places where I grew up, never bothered anyone here. The concept of time and space was entirely different. But I also learnt that in these territories, invisible to most Colombians, there was a more natural and powerful driving force, as well as a deeper sense of humanity.

During the day, I visited the communities along the riverbanks and the shores of the sea. I immersed myself in their lives, touring their territories and getting to know their families. However, I soon noticed an unsettling presence: outsiders engaged in illegal mining and coca cultivation. The unspoken rule was to look the other way; they followed their paths, and we followed ours. I found myself contemplating how the worlds of illegal and legal trade intersected in this territory. It pained me to witness the flourishing of illegal activities, thriving in the absence of state authority. This neglect allowed weapons and money to overshadow the dreams of these communities, whose lives, while simple, were far from miserable. The state's abandonment left a void that was dangerously filled by forces that threatened their way of life.

At night, we would gather outside to sing. For them, singing was as essential as breathing. Songsters would intone melodies to welcome the new day while cooking, fishing, planting, or building, and even when greeting a neighbor. In every situation—joyous or sorrowful—even at funerals, bidding farewell to the departed took the form of a chant.

Late at night, enchanting voices would echo through the forest, which looked majestic under the glow of the moonlight. It was a delight to listen to them sing the *aguabajo*—a distinctive rhythm from this region—accompanied by the guitar and marimba, with the unmistakable sound of the *guasa* joining in. The guasa, a traditional instrument from the Pacific coast, resembles a long, flat piece of wood, often filled with seeds or small pebbles that enhance its sound. The combination of the wooden body and the seeds creates a sharp yet resonant timbre, making the guasa an essential element of Afro-Colombian music. The women would remove their guasas from their satchels in unison, like hidden weapons ready for battle. They seemed to master the value of each grain nestled within the hollow trunks, which, when struck together, sounded like rhythmic splashes of rain. It was their weapon against sadness and abandonment. In those moments, I felt profoundly grateful to be in that place at that time.

One of the families with the most enduring musical tradition, the Angulos of San José, a village where I spent much of my time, sang an *aguabajo* (a traditional music rhythm) for me that filled my heart with joy. The title of the song was "Blossomed the Moon." As the tempo picked up, it flowed into other rhythms such as *currulao* and *juga*. The women whom I affectionately called "auntie" because I considered them as part of my family encouraged me just like my mother would: "Move your body, lift those feet of yours . . . please, move your body." There was something in the music of this place, its dance, its daily life that connected me deeply with nature and its vital force. I felt truly myself in this place, maybe because, in distancing myself from everything else, I had come closer to my own essence. I experienced an indescribable sense of freedom, joy, and being that was unlike anything I had ever known. Little by little, another Paula, or maybe the same one, began shedding her old layers, revealing her truest self.

I found myself captivated by the landscape, enchanted by the sight of its inhabitants paddling their boats to school, fishing for lunch, or visiting relatives. I remember climbing barefoot onto canoes and boats without a hint of fear, reveling in the sheer freedom of it all. My soaked feet embraced the coolness of the water as I felt the smooth pebbles, the rich texture of the mud, and the warm wood beneath me. In those moments, I learned the profound art of simplicity.

As I became more immersed in the lives of these communities, my role as a hyper-professional consultant was totally transformed. I found myself questioning what it truly meant to be a professional in such a context. The answer came from learning to trust, to go with the flow, and to let go of rigid structures. These riverine and forest communities became my greatest teachers, revealing a new sense of humanity to me. I was deeply transformed by their resilience, where Indigenous and Black people were like family to each other. To them, I was simply "Paula" and nothing more. They didn't care about my past or where I was headed.

In these communities, I learned the value of warmth extended to someone outside the immediate family but who becomes family through trust. This warmth was evident not only in their hospitality and food, but also in the music of their kisses and the strength of their hugs. This was especially true with the older women—each kiss had its own sound, from the more discreet and simple to the drawn-out "muaaah" of a joyful reunion. Their hugs, which felt like the ultimate chiropractic treatment, said something like "don't forget me" and "you belong here too."

Little did I know that just a few months after living among them, I would return—not as a visitor but as their minister.

Part V

The Power of Cinderella

In my early interviews and meetings, a recurring statement emerged: "Culture is the Cinderella." This phrase resonated deeply with me, especially since I had once come across a column titled "The Black Cinderella." I felt a haunting connection to this character, which illuminated an uncomfortable truth about the need to be taken seriously regarding one's value and importance, both ethnically and culturally. Unlike the traditional fairytale, there was no need for a transformation of clothes, no glass slippers, and no prince to chase for validation from the exclusive Colombian elites. The real challenge was to harness the unique power of culture and diversity, emphasizing their relevance and impact to secure the necessary support for growth and elevate them as national priorities.

Culture is often viewed as something self-evident, relegated to the decorative and secondary. Much like environmental and ethnic issues, there is a troubling ignorance surrounding the true meaning and significance of culture. This ignorance paves the way for perceptions riddled with stereotypes and simplistic views. What does culture signify in a country like Colombia? How do we define its value, actions, and actors beyond the self-proclaimed cultured groups? To move forward, we needed not only effective actions, we also needed to dig deep into the roots of these deeply entrenched beliefs. It was crucial to challenge these conceptions and elevate the discourse around culture, ensuring it received the attention and respect it deserved.

In Colombia, culture constitutes the spiritual and emotional infrastructure of the country; it is a glue that binds memories and expressions, capable of bringing together and stressing differences, of highlighting shared meanings and symbols. In moments of crises, artists and cultural leaders have contributed to building trust, strength, and hope in several sectors. Our culture is not one. Former minister and mentor Juan Luis

Mejía stressed that cultures are multiple, vital, dynamic, and intense and that they flourish by renewing and regenerating communal fabrics. Examples abound. Starting with the dance that frees up the spirit and constitutes the body of the nation; music that endows day-to-day life with rhythm, beckoning everyone to join in and raise their voices; literature that creates new worlds, making us wonder at a more profound and human reality; visual arts that depict the past and present, while suggesting a possible future in diversity of forms, abstractions, and colors.

In the depths of the cultural biographies of our country were hidden traces of great achievements as well as trails of conflicts, potential developments, and great misunderstandings, including our deepest resentments and frustrations. Sometimes what comes off as most evident or as closest to our common experiences turns out to be the most difficult to explain. One debate that came up was how to double the budget, right in the middle of a financial crisis and budgetary cuts. The strategy was to expand the sources of finance through laws with permanent economic incentives in tandem with a record flow of national and international cooperation resources. At that time, all was geared toward demonstrating that lack of investment in the domain of culture constituted a drawback for the national agenda and to stress that such an investment was nothing less than imperative. It was also fundamental to remind those in decision-making positions of the tangible impact of culture in their own lives. For instance, think of that specific book that completely changed your understanding of a specific subject matter, that piece of music that raised you to an emotional state of conviviality, among myriad other key daily experiences that have transformed the way we all appreciate our existence.

During one Ministerial Council meeting, I argued that just as road infrastructure was critical for national competitiveness, cultural initiatives are critical for collective meanings. It was what my good friend Gilberto Gil called *infovías* and what I referred to as "the emotional infrastructure of the country." Our mission was not only to fight material poverty but also to address the poverty of collective meaning and creativity, which arises from the lack of quality investments and dignified cultural infrastructures. I am not sure if my words truly resonated, but at the very least, they sparked a debate about the power and transcendence of culture.

Chapter 14

The Ministry of Diversity

Several years ago, during a conference in Canning House, London, I declared that ministries of culture are in effect ministries of memory, diversity, and equality. I went forward to state that the duty of a Minister of Culture is to bring societies together, not in spite of, but thanks to their differences. I gave the example of Colombia, where you have such extremely different regions like the Caribbean, the Pacific, the Andes, the Plains, and the Amazonas in the same country. A country of contrasts, made up of thick forests, plains with limitless horizons, and clean air moors; of snow mountains and deserts inhabited by ethnic groups with their bright colored covers; of forested beaches in the Pacific as well as multicolor Caribbean waters; of islands and mangroves, without forgetting the hectic urban centers. In short, a series of parallel worlds, spanning from the creole community in San Andrés Island to the Wayuu territory or the ancestral lands of the Sierra Nevada or of the Pira Paraná in Vaupés. A coffee universe unfolds in stark contrast to the Estoraques landscape of Northern Santander, where striking rock formations and towering cliffs rise dramatically from the earth. This juxtaposition highlights the rich diversity of Colombia's geography, with the lush, rolling hills of coffee plantations giving way to the surreal, rugged beauty of nature's sculptures. A multiethnic country born out of racial mixture, with more than eighty different Indigenous groups, Afro-Colombian, Hispanic, and Arab-descendant communities and heritage present in our cultural biographies. Sixty-eight native languages (sixty-five of which are Indigenous, two Afro-descendant—Creole and Palenquera—and Romani), which, together with Spanish, enrich the universe of our structures of thoughts and meaning-making. A fatherland of municipalities with multivocal names such as Amalfi, Aranzazu, Piendamó, Mutatá, or

Usiacurí. A country of dissimilar regions, with immense environmental and cultural diversity.

Being a Black minister gave me a unique perspective on how difference was considered exclusively as something extraneous and exotic. To be different meant to belong to this large and assorted mass of people who feature in history and in the news media in a cursory, biased, and uncontextualized manner. For this reason, the understanding of the different other is a profoundly ethical issue, which speaks of humanity in its rather encompassing sense, conscious of each person's diversity in one aspect or another. My mission was to give expression not only to the closed circle of a few self-declared enlightened elites, but also to convert the Ministry of Culture into the Ministry of Diversity, open and dynamic, available to the excluded as well. It was no longer a matter of "you and us" but rather an all-inclusive and diverse "we."

In December 2007, I spent my first Christmas as a minister, immersed in the vibrant atmosphere of Granada (Meta) for the annual meeting of the National Music Plan. More than five hundred young musicians gathered in a sweltering coliseum, and I felt a surge of excitement at the prospect of celebrating the season with music and young talent. As the ceremony began, the first group performed Christmas carols, including a spirited rendition of "Jingle Bells." My attention was drawn to a group of men in cowboy hats and black ceremonial suits, while the little girls, dressed in white and adorned with flowers, stood out beautifully. Yet I was puzzled by their choice of foreign songs, as they assured me that folk music would come later. I found it contradictory that these local performers viewed their own traditions as secondary, despite their pursuit of excellence in symphonic music. After half an hour, I urged them to embrace their roots. When the harp and cuatros began to play, the audience swayed to the joropo's lively rhythm, and I was filled with an overwhelming sense of joy. The music transported me to the vast plains, rich with cowboy culture and heritage. As the last notes faded, I felt overwhelmed by the vitality of the moment. The celebration culminated with a captivating chirimía performance from two schools of Chocó. A group of children in orange trousers and white floral shirts created a dazzling spectacle with their drums and clarinets. The blend of colors and sounds symbolized the beautiful fusion of our diverse identities.

Immediately upon returning to Bogotá, I felt compelled to act. I requested the team of the National Music Plan to strengthen the diversity of musical practices across the country, elevating traditional music forms like the marimba, chirimía, and gaitas, as well as urban music alongside symphonic music. We needed more scores, more songbooks—more of what is authentically ours—so that the vibrant sounds of our culture could resonate far and wide at the same level of excellence and recognition of more globalized music traditions.

Chapter 15

"Culture Opened Up"

This was the headline under which our U-turn began to gain media attention, a banner that guided our tours across various territories. It became increasingly clear that some of our deepest exclusions were rooted in cultural perceptions—particularly in what people deemed to be culture. We needed to shift this narrative.

To address these issues, we launched a monthly series of talks titled "Culture for All," in which key ministry members would visit crucial, often isolated municipalities to assess our actions and omissions in the field. Our first trip in June took us to Buenaventura on the Pacific coast. I was deeply moved by a group of enthusiastic young people who told me, "You look just like us, and seeing how much you've achieved gives us hope." Yet, when I asked them about their dreams, they responded starkly: "In this port, nothing good has ever happened and nothing ever will." Their words hit me hard, revealing just how deep the challenges ran. This visit helped us define our agenda, resulting in at least five concrete and exemplary projects that would serve as visible markers of my legacy.

When I first took office, I received many congratulatory messages and went through each and every one of them. The most touching of them came from the ethnic communities and people in prisons. Most of the Indigenous community leaders began visiting my office, leaving behind symbols of friendship such as the baton of command and hand-carved masks. In one of the letters written by the spiritual authorities of the Indigenous communities of La Chorrera in the Amazon, they requested for the Casa Arana to be recognized as a national heritage site. La Casa Arana was the emblematic flashpoint of the holocaust perpetrated against the Indigenous people in that region at the turn of the twentieth century. That place bears witness to the torture, death, and extermination of more than eighty thousand Indigenous people in a genocide perpetrated in the process of rubber exploitation. José Eustasio Rivera recounts this tragedy in his book, *The Vortex* (1924), in which the inhospitable nature of the forest is dwarfed by utter human perverseness whereby, motivated by economic greed, man enslaves fellow man without the least sense of humanity as the rest of country turns a blind eye. It was clear that I had to visit.

After my inaugural visit to Buenaventura, my team and I boarded a three-hour flight on a Colombian Air Force aircraft that delivered monthly supplies to the heart of the Amazon. Upon landing, we were greeted by children waving Colombian flags. It was a powerful moment, a chance to affirm that they represented the essence of Colombia—strong, Indigenous, generous, and resilient. These children symbolized a community determined to reclaim their space from the horrors of Casa Arana, standing firm to honor their ancestors and build a brighter future. As the Uruguayan writer Eduardo Galeano wisely says, "Living memory was not born to serve as an anchor but rather as a steppingstone."

After disembarking, we began a twenty-minute walk to the meeting place. The sky darkened ominously, and soon the rain began to pour. As we approached, the Irana-Paraná River came into view, its powerful waterfall reverberating in the air—a fitting introduction to the magical place known as La Chorrera. The locals spoke of this waterfall with reverence, claiming it embodied the strength of the gods, with its heart holding the energy of the world. It was a sacred site, the birthplace of the sacred beings who had shaped creation itself. This hallowed ground is home to four Indigenous ethnic communities—the Uitotos, Boras, Ocarinas, and Muinane—who proudly identify as the progeny of tobacco, coca, and sweet cassava. Drenched yet determined, we arrived at the house that had once been a symbol of domination and atrocity. This two-story, khaki-colored wooden structure now housed a community college known as the House of Knowledge. The first floor still held the remnants of a darker past, with rooms that had once served as sites for extracting rubber and torturing Indigenous communities. Casa Arana stood as a haunting reminder of sorrow, where the weight of history lingered even amid the glimmers of hope. We ascended to the second floor, where we shared cassava bread and coffee. As the rain gave way to sunshine, the ceremony commenced. My team observed, absorbed in the moment. Here, it was not about lecturing on diversity; it was about engaging directly with the people, cultivating a sense of mutual responsibility that transcended words.

Then came the time for the rites, vibrant with color and rich in texture, each detail imprinted on skin and attire. Adorned with feathers atop their heads, fibers woven into skirts and gowns, and seeds dangling from their feet, the men and women began to dance. Initially, they moved in circles, but soon divided into two groups, one for men and one for women, facing each other in a display of unity and tradition. As the dance unfolded, the air filled with the resonant chants of the men, their voices rising in powerful harmony. A millenary tree, nearly thirty-two feet tall, lay on the ground, serving as a percussion instrument for the traditional songs. Twelve men sang in unison, their feet striking the trunk with a dry, resonant thud that marked the rhythm. It was the beat of a warrior song, a hymn of resistance. In their language, this sound embodied a chorus of militant voices, echoing the strength of a struggle that had persisted for more than a century. This moment was not just a performance; it was a testament to their enduring spirit.

From there we walked for a while around the village. The caciques and the wise men of the community were waiting for me at the *maloca*, the sacred space that stood for the belly and was believed to be the cradle of the world. For the Indigenous communities, the maloca is the place to free the heart and cleanse the spirit. It is a circular and open structure, with a woven roof, apparently too large for its low-lying walls. As soon as we made our entry, the elders asked me to sit on one of the tree trunks close to them. I was just about to deliver a speech when they told me, "You have come here to listen to us; we have gathered here so as to put our thoughts together to make sure everything goes well with you." They stressed the sacred value of the word in the maloca, adding that what you profess with your mouth in the maloca must be accompanied by your actions. Everyone needed to pay heed to what was uttered there, and if any pact was concluded, it absolutely had to be honored. Another cacique looked at me and said, "We would like to let you know what culture is. Culture refers to the roots of this tree; the tree is Colombia. If the roots are not properly preserved, maintained, and if they are not well nourished, in no way will the tree grow and bear fruits. If these roots are not strong and firm enough, the tree will not grow adequately."

They bid me farewell with a heartfelt promise: whenever they gathered in the maloca, they would raise their thoughts to the spirits of nature on my behalf. At that moment, I shared my plans for the future, and they responded, "Ideas will begin to dawn." Indeed, in the first year of my tenure, I witnessed a blossoming of both ideas and understanding, alongside a deepening passion to serve. I felt a profound and ancestral connection to these spiritual authorities, who had guided their community in achieving a miracle of cultural perpetuity despite the looming threat of extermination. Today, that threat persists—not through the extraction of rubber, but through drug trafficking, mineral exploitation, and illegal logging. Their resilience continues to inspire me and surrounds me to this day.

Chapter 16

The Dawn of New Ideas

On November 24, 2007, just thirteen days after my twenty-ninth birthday and six months into my role as Minister, I found myself seated between Mexican President Felipe Calderón and four literary luminaries of Latin America: Gabriel García Márquez, Carlos Fuentes, Fernando del Paso, and Álvaro Mutis. Surrounded by thousands, including hundreds of national and international media correspondents, I was at the official opening of the Guadalajara Book Fair, the most significant literary event in Latin America. Colombia was the guest country, and my predecessor had assembled a remarkable delegation of more than four hundred members. This event was not just a highlight on my agenda; it was my baptism by fire.

That morning I woke up determined to be optimistic, telling myself that everything would be alright. I reassured myself that everything had been prepared—every detail checked, every space visited. My only tasks were to feel confident, review my speech, and remember that, regardless of my personal feelings, I was the spokeswoman for a nation. I chose a white dress, symbolizing serenity, allowing me to appear radiant without drawing too much attention. As I dressed, I took a moment to examine myself in the mirror. Despite my efforts to breathe deeply and relax, my reflection revealed a deep-seated fear. I applied some makeup and styled my hair, striving to present myself in the best possible light. Yet I felt invisible, lost in the mirror, somewhat anesthetized by the moment. I desperately needed to overcome the nervousness that was evident in my trembling hands as they struggled to grasp the envelope I had chosen as my handbag.

Soon the organizers came to escort me to the event. I hurriedly reviewed all the details for the opening and took a moment to go over my printed speech once more. Shortly after, I stepped outside, repeating to myself that everything would be alright. Upon arriving at the auditorium, I was ushered to the table of honor, facing thousands of attendees. Some Colombians in the audience noticed my anxiety and smiled encouragingly, while others watched skeptically. I sat at a rectangular table adorned with an elegant white tablecloth.

The first to arrive was Gabo, accompanied by Álvaro Mutis. Soon after, Fernando del Paso and Carlos Fuentes entered. The last to arrive was President Felipe Calderón, accompanied by his delegation. Sensing my nervousness, Gabo leaned over and whispered, "You represent us very well; be calm." We had first met in May of that same year during his return to his hometown of Aracataca. He had invited me on a special train trip, where he kept insisting, "And they claim Macondo does not exist." I had also visited him at his home in Mexico City, in the space he called "The Conspiracy Room," where we discussed my progress and the state of the country. I had asked him to lead the Colombian delegation in Guadalajara and to pay tribute to his dear friend and confidant, the poet Álvaro Mutis.

The Book Fair was officially opened, and I was called upon as the first speaker. The earth trembled beneath my feet, and my body felt heavier than usual. I froze for a moment, but Gabo took my hand. I stepped up to the podium, his thumb raised in encouragement. I began my speech with the words, "I come this evening as a grateful reader, and because Colombia is fond of Mexico." I wasn't there as a literary expert reciting eloquent phrases from advisors; I have always believed in the power of written words to unlock a world of experiences, guided by an inner voice that deepens as the writer invites the reader to embark on a journey of self-discovery.

We read and write to be, to understand, to create meaning, to imagine, to negotiate our space and time, our memories, and our dreams. This process triggers specific ways of filling our thoughts, our feelings, and ultimately shaping our conscience. For this reason, this meeting was fundamentally important to me. Not only was I representing one of the cornerstones of Colombian culture, but I was also speaking to myself as a future emerging writer—one who has published two books and been a columnist for major Colombian newspapers for fifteen years.

I love to read, but one of my main passions is writing the words that will speak for me when I am no longer in this world. No one will speak for me without me. In my speech, I also emphasized the special relationship between Colombia and Mexico. Mexico has been home to many of our great authors, who found a solid foundation here to grow and transcend. Finally, I highlighted how Mexico's daily presence in our music, television, and popular imagination is truly remarkable.

Years later, in 2011, I was honored by President Felipe Calderón with the Order of the Aztec Eagle, the highest distinction from the Mexican government, in recognition of my contributions to increasing cooperation and exchanges between Mexico and Colombia. During this period, Mexican Ambassador Florencio Salazar and I became great friends and built a robust agenda to further connect our countries. After the Book Fair, we were guests of honor at the Festival Cervantino, where we attended film festivals and exhibitions, creating a fruitful exchange. Everything went well, and overcoming that moment significantly boosted my self-confidence.

I must say that Gabo's encouragement meant a great deal to me. Once, when I requested his autograph, he signed it: "Your servant." As such an iconic figure, he had a remarkable ability to connect with and support someone like me, whom he barely knew. After our wide-ranging conversations, he would often ask, "Paula, how is the man doing?" followed by a hearty laugh. His humor and informality created an atmosphere that touched the heart before delving into our political discussions. I found his creative works fascinating, particularly his portrayal of the hidden beauty of the Caribbean, which is often difficult to define. He defied many intellectual categories to carve out a space for reflection from the margins in a country known for its centralism. His in-depth depictions of local and national power elites enhanced our understanding of how power operates in a complex and tumultuous society like Colombia. Gabo was, and shall remain, the most global of Colombians—someone who will continue to challenge our memory forever.

Reflecting on my own journey as Minister, which was just starting in Mexico, I served for three years and six months—more than one thousand days, to be precise, including the thirty days before my official announcement. It felt much longer, not only because of the intensity of the experiences but also due to the beauty and grandeur of our accomplishments. Yet the complexity and challenges were ever present, always lurking in the background. During my tenure, I visited all thirty-two departments of the country and traveled to 300 of the 1,126 municipalities.

We passed new laws on native languages, tangible and intangible heritage, and libraries, alongside state policies for cultural industries, a national audiovisual and dance plan, and historic centers. Two laws remained unfinished—one on public performances and another on music—which I had to leave for my successors due to time constraints. We successfully increased the budget and expanded our cooperative efforts. Duty called us to visit prisons, military bases, orchestras, and hip-hop collectives, ensuring that there was a program and a response to the diverse cultural experiences across Colombia. Our country was the guest of honor at more than twenty international events, and we issued national and international recognitions of cultural landmarks. Even when time was short, we never relented.

On average, I spent only three to four days a week in Bogotá. My mornings at the office began at six, with the first hour dedicated to reading documents, responding to emails, and preparing for the day's meetings, which started at seven. These meetings involved collaborating with my team to co-create or follow up on various initiatives in detail and working with key partners such as other government agencies, local secretaries of culture, international diplomats, or cooperation agencies. In the afternoons, I held meetings with congress members or personally visited Congress to advocate for budget increases or the approval of specific laws. Evenings were reserved for attending award ceremonies, exhibition openings, or book and concert launches. Managing my time accurately and setting priorities in a very organized agenda was critical for my effectiveness.

During one of my trips, I had the opportunity to spend time with a group of female prisoners who were participating in a program we developed called Freedom Under the Word, where they were being trained to become librarians. This initiative was built around the need for libraries and literature workshops in all penitentiary centers. Many detainees wrote to me, expressing the importance of this program and my visits to the prisons. Committed to this cause, I made it a point to visit the penitentiary center once a month.

My visits often began with a reading from *Fugas de Tinta* (Ink Leakage), a collection of texts written by inmates from across the country. One passage by Ricardo Jiménez reads: "Even if we are indexed as the dregs of society, I am an example of the fact that there are people here full of faith and willing to change, to fight for our society, and to attest to the reality that each one of us, at some point in our lives, is bound to commit mistakes. These mistakes do not entirely define who we are, our capacities, or our virtues."

During each visit, I shared reflections from Malcolm X on how prisons, through access to reading, can become places where individuals channel their struggles and discover the foundations of their ethnic and spiritual identity. After my time in the prison, I would rush to a nearby cultural center or recording studio in the local community. At noon, I often had lunch with a mayor or another local authority, aiming to build alliances and secure additional resources. By the end of the day, I would return to Bogotá, holding a follow-up meeting with my team—whether in the waiting room or any informal space—to review our commitments and set clear timelines for various tasks. It was essential to me that what we promised was diligently followed through.

Time flew by, and before I realized it, I was entering my second year in office, which would kick off with the commemoration of Independence Day. For this event, we decided to shift the focus away from the traditional military parade, which had always been central to the celebrations. We asked ourselves why, nearly two centuries later, weapons were still seen as a modern symbol of freedom, especially in a country with such a complex history of violence. It was essential for us to give new meaning to social mobilization and to emphasize the civil values of independence and liberty.

Colombian music, with its vibrant artists, became the ideal medium for rallying and nurturing a sense of unity and diversity. With this vision in mind, we organized the Grand National Concert on July 20, transforming Independence Day into a celebration of our cultural richness. We successfully coordinated more than a thousand music concerts simultaneously across the nation and abroad, establishing an annual tradition that brought together more than two hundred thousand artists and attracted more than ten million Colombians—whether gathered in plazas or watching live broadcasts from their homes. Our collaboration with both public and private media ensured that the Grand Concert reached a wide audience, showcasing renowned Colombian figures like Shakira, Carlos Vives, and Juanes, while also honoring music legends such as Jorge Villamil, Joe Arroyo, and Jairo Varela, the founder of Grupo Niche, to whom I awarded the highest order of the minister. I also celebrated Rafael Cassiani from San

Basilio de Palenque, with his marímbula, and cherished the rehearsals with Cholo Valderrama in his home, where we played harp music from the plains.

The motivation behind this initiative came from acknowledging the humanity and struggles of countless artists who act as cultural ambassadors. Additionally, we prioritized emerging talents and music schools, allowing them to share the stage with these renowned stars, creating a vibrant tapestry of sound. Together, we crafted a beautiful symphony that enriched the country's soundtrack year after year. This mobilization of music not only became a hallmark of my term but also represented a symbolic achievement, showcasing the tangible results of our national music plan as we neared the bicentennial celebration.

The inaugural Grand Concert took place in the heart of the Amazon, in Leticia, marking a significant milestone in our cultural celebration. Attended by three heads of state—Peru's Alan García, Brazil's Luis Inácio Lula da Silva, and Colombia's Álvaro Uribe—the event featured performances by stars like Shakira and Carlos Vives, drawing an audience of over eighty thousand. The concert began with the Colombian national anthem sung in the Tikuna language by indigenous elders from the maloca of Moroapu, accompanied by a youth symphonic orchestra. This powerful moment was the result of extensive negotiations within the organizing committee, particularly regarding the live TV broadcast. It was essential to us that our hosts be recognized by millions of viewers. Our first message was that Colombia is home to not only Spanish but also sixty-eight indigenous languages, with more than eighty different indigenous ancestral cultures laying the foundation of our country. After an intense negotiation, we successfully ensured that the elders would open the concert, setting the tone for this meaningful celebration.

My team and I traveled to Moroapu, Puerto Nariño, several days before the event to meet with the elders. On the day of the concert, they felt understandably hesitant to step onto the podium, overwhelmed by the large crowd. They only agreed to perform after my team and I promised to join them on stage, singing the national anthem in the Tikuna language alongside them, which we had learned through multiple rehearsal sessions. Following the anthem, the heads of state made brief welcoming remarks from the podium reserved for dignitaries. The elders had prepared gifts for the presidents, Shakira, and Carlos Vives. As we stepped down from the stage together, they sought to present their gifts to these esteemed guests. However, I was informed by the security team that the elders were not allowed on the presidential podium. Astonished by this restriction, I made it clear that if they were denied access, I would not step up either. I stood firm with the elders until I was called by the president, and I came up with them. It was a powerful moment to witness as the presidents and cultural icons knelt to receive gifts from local Indigenous authorities. This scene became another symbolic gesture of our ongoing quest for cultural equality: we all build the country, we all share the podium, and we all deserve and receive the recognition for our diverse contributions.

My second year as minister began with a marathon of events, meetings, and countless flights, filled with intense activity and the forging of numerous connections. I was not only preparing legislation to present to Congress but also launching new national plans aimed at creating systemic, rather than just symbolic, change. This whirlwind of activity continued throughout my tenure, with each year marked by an overwhelming schedule that left little time for rest. I led ten major discussions at the presidency, faced four attempts at resignation, and managed only two brief holiday periods. I spent a hundred weekends in my office and endured several attacks. The rapid and complex nature of my responsibilities made it difficult to fully grasp the magnitude of the impact—the vastness of the country, the diversity of experiences, and the rich exchange of life that took place throughout this journey.

Chapter 17

The Ministry of Peace

There was never enough time to accomplish all I had envisioned for the Ministry of Culture. One of my key aspirations was to show how the Ministry could effectively serve as the Ministry of Peace, embodying a profound and genuine peace that fosters reconciliation. I imagined a pilot project focused on rural women who were victims of violence, beginning with the Pacific region and its women's organizations. This project aimed to strengthen the therapeutic role of culture, build networks of solidarity, and enhance the expressive capacities of communities in need of healing, helping them to process their pain and envision a hopeful future.

Less than a year before the end of my tenure, I traveled to Tumaco to assess the progress of the Marimba Pathways project and to meet with leaders of women's organizations. I wanted to understand their experiences and evaluate the training, the processes, and the challenges they had encountered. I arrived on the second floor of the house of one of the members of the local committee of the women's group, where eight women leaders were waiting for me. Each of them took turns to tell the story of their life before, during, and after the conflict. The common thread was the fact that they had all been forced to abandon their communities after their partners were murdered, escaping with only their children and eyes filled with tears, without even the chance to look back. No funerals, no goodbyes, just the urgency to protect their children. In the blink of an eye, they left everything behind. I listened in silence, trying to grasp the depth of their suffering.

When they finished, I realized how isolated they were, cut off from society, often seen as collaborators with armed groups, while their children faced limited life options, vulnerable to being recruited by criminal organizations. They shared stories of resistance: how they would lock their kids at home, hungry, while they went out in search for food. I felt utterly helpless. For the first time in a long while, I broke down in tears. One of the women noticed my distress and said to the others, "The minister is so sad; we have to cheer her up." To my surprise, they started singing and smiling. One of them stood up and held me tightly. At that moment, I thought, "How is this possible? I am the one who is supposed to console them. But instead, they turn out to be the ones comforting me." Here, in this small room, was the crucible of peacebuilding in our country—a space where women who had lived through the worst of the conflict were finding ways to heal, to ensure their sons would not become tomorrow's killers. I would have loved to spend more time with them, to engage in a more encompassing project with these women, but I was quickly running out of time.

Chapter 18

Paula or the Minister?

Where does the personal end and the official begin? My time as minister was so intense that on February 28, 2008, I wrote in my diary:

> There are days like this when life becomes a heavy burden and one is confronted with human nature. There are moments when everything feels like a struggle, even a piece of paper . . . Contradictions, limitations, moments. At the end, that is life, with its silences. At times, I feel so turned outward that I find it difficult to focus inward. Should I leave? Where is that happy place where life feels unified and whole? I don't know. Should I leave? Or should I stay? I don't know for sure. I don't know. I am no longer the same person and there are certain things that make me deeply sad, but what would that mean for people who have accompanied me all long?

Being a minister demanded radical changes in my life. At first, I struggled to adjust to the role. I was often scared to face certain challenges and situations and developed the habit of praying before making any decision. I would wake up very early and go to bed quite late, pouring over documents, profiles, projects, and any other sources, trying to prepare for each meeting as best as I could. Every situation felt like a moment of reckoning.

In the early months, I had no time to rest. The days flew by, and I had to start waking up at four in the morning to squeeze in more time for reading and reflection, staying up until midnight. From four to five, I would immerse myself in various texts on culture. Then I spent the next forty-five minutes tidying up so as to be in the office at six o'clock in the morning. During the first few months, I worked every weekend. On Sundays, I would arrive at the office by eight in the morning and dedicate the entire day to reading contracts and correspondence. This was my way of preparing for any potential legal issues or lawsuits related to my duties. My mother, being a lawyer, had offered me guidance on handling processes that could cause complications down the line.

At the same time, some people within the ministry tried to sabotage my efforts. They spread rumors to the media, the presidency, and other channels, hoping to discredit me. For example, one morning I was called onto one of the country's most popular radio talk shows and asked, quite bluntly, why I had supposedly requested a fleet of twenty cars for my family and myself. I responded with the simple truth: I had never asked for any cars. I only had the three vehicles assigned to me, including the security escort from my predecessor, and another car for a family member, as was standard for any minister. Why on earth would I need such a large fleet?

During that same program, I faced about ten more questions, all based on rumors and baseless accusations. What struck me as most curious was that, according to my advisers, many offices in the ministry were tuned in to that radio broadcast at the time. In such a hostile environment, it was clear that not only were some people hoping I would fail, but they were also actively working to make it happen by pushing me to make as many errors as possible, and I had to be extremely cautious. I meticulously reviewed every letter, speech, communiqué, and contract to avoid any missteps. It felt like navigating a minefield, but as long as I remained fully aware of what was happening under my watch, I could prevent unpleasant surprises.

Another challenge was managing my public image. I had to spend time visiting several designers, make-up artists, hairdressers, and even models to curate my appearance as a public figure. To be honest, I never gave much thought to my wardrobe or to my image, but I quickly realized that it was essential to present myself well, from avoiding the same outfit appearing in every newspaper to understanding the importance of a polished appearance in front of the cameras. Every little detail mattered: what I wore, how I looked at the camera, even my hairstyle and the way I walked. I had to be mindful of all these aspects.

During the first few months, even years, I often felt like I was wearing a disguise. When I looked in the mirror, I would struggle to recognize myself.

The photos in the newspapers sometimes portrayed me as a refined lady, other times very plump. Some days my face carried a sparkle; other days, it seemed like an enemy had done my make-up. Occasionally, my hair was poorly groomed. Some people suggested I wear accessories, like jewels and wristwatches, but I did not give in. The truth is that I have always been psychologically allergic to the feeling of being overloaded, fastened up, encumbered, or shackled, and that is exactly how I felt under the weight of jewels. I have always preferred to wear just earrings. Finding the right style wasn't easy, and it's something I'm still refining today. I learned that you don't need to pretend to be something you are not or someone you do not feel like being. You just have to be aware that people will judge you based on your appearance; even if they do not know you, they often will not take the time to understand who you really are. Each time I flipped through pictures from those bygone days, year after year, I noticed how much my external appearance mirrored the internal changes I was going through. Each year I felt stronger and more comfortable in my role. As I grew more confident, I started using brighter colors, higher heels, and eventually stopped hiding behind the jackets I often used to conceal my body. I learned to enjoy the process of rediscovering and re-creating my image through my clothing, always making a conscious effort to remain true to myself in all of that.

My health became an issue as well. The day I turned twenty-nine—almost six months after taking office—I spent my birthday under medical care. I, who had rarely experienced any health issues, suddenly found myself, after a few months of medical exams, dealing with a range of illnesses—from hypoglycemia to high uric acid and elevated cholesterol levels. My body was responding to the intense pressure I was under. I realized I needed to take better care of myself and manage challenging situations more wisely. In response, I made the decision to avoid most night events, except for those hosted by ambassadors or important award ceremonies, so I could get an extra hour or two of sleep by going to bed earlier. I also made sure to rest one or two Sundays a month.

Feeling vulnerable because of my health compelled me, at the same time, to deal with my fears as best as I could. I sought to identify what triggered my tension and made a conscious effort to reassure myself, telling myself over and over that everything would be fine. At the same time, I leaned on two or three people in whom I could absolutely trust and opened up to them daily on how I was feeling. One other thing that made me conquer my multiple fears and insecurities was the resolution not to do anything with the aim of impressing anyone, but rather to act according to my conscience, without exaggerating neither my successes nor my failures and to accept that to err is human. I kept learning as the days went by that the first and foremost person I needed to convince and satisfy by my actions was none other than myself.

Being in the spotlight comes at a very high cost—whether delivering keynote speeches, serving as the guest of honor, or holding a position of distinction, there was a constant demand to strike the right balance. I had to find the rightful median as to when to be formal and when to be informal, when to be spontaneous and when to be diplomatic, when to set boundaries and when to assert my authority, when to persuade and when to take a firmer stance. But it was also difficult to read the minds of others, to ascertain their references and intentions, which made me cautious about not appearing unprepared in my interactions with them. I found it hard to assess every word and to make a strategic analysis of how my words could subsequently be used against me. I also felt that my performance represented not just myself but also an entire community.

It was also uncomfortable to feel that I was constantly on trial, being evaluated. I often had the sensation of being out of place, learning to stay on the sidelines—present but distant—so as not to be affected by external pressures. I only felt at home among local communities, in the field.

At times, the vertigo I was experiencing provided fertile ground for several aspects of my personality to exacerbate. Sometimes I would not go through everything thoroughly, yet I expected perfection and quick resolution. I became deeply frustrated whenever things did not turn out the way I intended, and though I didn't want to come across as someone hardened by the pressures of work, I sometimes felt that way. In those moments, it proved very helpful for me to always leave my door open to members of my team and other people to lend them a listening ear. What mattered to me was letting the entire team know that having come with me this far, they were an integral part of the project we were striving to accomplish together. I lowered my guard, and instead of referring to them as "you," I preferred to say "we."

As a minister, I lost my sense of privacy, and many issues proved quite new to me. To begin with, the security team assigned to me was made up of six men, two drivers and four bodyguards, who accompanied me everywhere I went. I had to move about in an armored vehicle, with dark windows, led by another car that cleared the way, poised to be the first to react in the case of any emergency. I found it hard to get comfortable with the fact that everywhere I arrived was already subjected to a prior security check or to be surrounded by bodyguards when strolling in the streets or when merely going to a nearby shop. I ended up developing great respect for those security guards, given that we spent about 70 percent of our time together. But, without doubt, those who enjoyed it were my nephews. They felt like they were watching the unfolding of a movie.

One evening I wanted to go out with Wolfgang, someone very special to me. We put everything together so we could sneak out without security to a restaurant in the suburbs of Bogotá. We left the garage, making sure that no one saw us, and arrived at a very little-known locality. There we were in the restaurant at the outskirts with less than ten tables, in the middle of the mountains, a very discreet place. But then came the surprise: when I arrived back home, I received a call from the presidency telling me I should not attempt to go to any place without security guards. After several attempts, I realized that the only time I could move about without security and without fear was when I traveled abroad or stayed at home.

Security became a matter of concern as much for my family as for me. I was eager to travel across the entire country to see firsthand if what we were planning or implementing was truly making an impact. It was certainly a hard time for the security team because I did not fully grasp the risks, nor did I feel any fear about visiting any municipality or locality. I did not keep my distance and whenever I stepped foot in the communities, I was filled with delight: I greeted everyone, people waved at me from their windows and invited me into their homes and I entered without a second thought. I found myself strolling in the most difficult neighborhoods, riding motorcycles, and getting into boats, for instance. I forgot that my position made me a military target given the armed conflict in Colombia. With a near-naive determination, I was committed to visiting every corner of the country, especially if the community was isolated or had never been visited by a minister before. Sometimes, just when I had everything carefully planned, on the day before, or during the visit, or the day after, the village would be seized by the guerrillas. Once, while visiting a municipality, gunfire rang out nearby, and my security detail had to throw me to the ground. On more than three occasions, I had to change course and time, or simply take a helicopter flight because explosives had been found on the road I was supposed to take, or someone was arrested for passing along information about the car I would be traveling in.

Despite these dangers, my desire to connect with the communities and understand their realities firsthand was stronger than any fear, and I continued my visits even in the most remote and conflict-prone areas. My mother constantly said to me, "Paula, take care, please take care," and I recall telling her, "Mum, what gives meaning to life, gives meaning to death, and I promised them." However, it is one thing to risk your own life and completely another to put the lives of others at risk. In time, I came to realize that, beyond the person, the role itself imposed certain rules. This understanding made me much more rigorous about following security protocols, as I didn't want to unnecessarily endanger the lives of my bodyguards and my team.

I think this constitutes one of the most difficult aspects of public life, not less so in a country like Colombia, where, more than five decades of war have led to more than two hundred thousand deaths, eighty thousand disappearances, and four million displaced people. At the time of my tenure (2007–2010), the guerrilla forces still boasted more than fifteen thousand members, excluding the criminal groups. Even if I did not want to pay attention to these figures, I had to adapt to the reality of constant security measures.

Another daily challenge was the need to be available by phone twenty-four hours a day. I'm naturally a bit forgetful, often leaving my phone behind or misplacing it. Now I was expected to always keep both my personal cell phone and the presidential phone with me, which added to my stress. Ironically, the president always seemed to call just when I didn't have the phone on hand. Whenever I heard the phone ring, a flood of anxious thoughts would race through my mind: "Who could it be?" "Did I miss something important?" "Did I forget to attend an event or overlook something crucial?" In the split second before answering, countless questions would rush through my head, adding to the pressure of the moment.

To my loved ones, it became clear that having a family member as minister of culture was not something easy to bear. A series of implicit pressures made it difficult to explain to one's friends and acquaintances who could not render favors nor undertake any kind of endeavors. My family thought it wise to keep its distance in the face of my ministerial duties. Everyone in the family knew too well that it was a historic opportunity not to be missed on account of trivial details.

My daily life continued to be populated with new acquaintances and novel realities. The time was gone when I could freely attend to my own affairs, such as going to the movies and shopping. In general, everyday matters and personal activities were now relegated to the background. I started reappropriating my former spaces little by little. I have always loved salsa, and before, it didn't matter where I went or with whom I danced. But about a month into my new role, I went out dancing in Cali and found myself unsure of who my dance partners were. After dancing with two strangers, I decided to leave—it was too uncomfortable.

For a while it was quite hard for me to explain it properly to my friends and my family: that I had to be more reserved in my social interactions and could no longer live a carefree, unguarded life. Over time, I returned to my favorite places, but with a new approach. I decided that I would only dance with people I knew and would frequent discos where I was familiar with the owners. In these familiar settings, I could relax and enjoy myself again, practicing my salsa moves while staying updated on the latest songs in town. As for drinking, liquor has never really been my thing. Occasionally I would have a glass of wine, but I made a point to avoid shots, even during my time at the ministry. The reason was simple: I just did not like it. I always wanted to be fully aware of my actions, and I could not predict how alcohol might affect me, so I preferred to stay in control.

Chapter 19

The Companion

The year 2013 was the year my cousin and sister, Patricia, passed away. That same year, I found myself in my pearl-gray van with her eight-year-old son, Esteban. This little Black boy, strong and sly with a mischievous smile, reaching my elbows, had become my biggest concern. His mum, my sister, was gone, and he and his two sisters had meant the world to her. That weekend, I decided to take him out for a walk to buy some books, visit a restaurant, chat, and run a few errands. Our conversation began with a series of questions:

> "Auntie, is it true that my mum will reincarnate?" Esteban asked.
>
> "I can't say for sure, Esteban," I replied.
>
> "And if that were the case, would she come back as a newborn?" he pressed.
>
> "I have no idea," I insisted gently.
>
> "Auntie, imagine the next baby I meet says, 'Hello, my son!'"
>
> "What a scare that would be!"

I burst into nervous laughter, picturing what the scene might truly look like. He had a clearer understanding of death than I did—seeing it as the ability to transform, where someone vanishes but then becomes vital energy in a new form, moving on. He knew that his mother had taken a different path and believed we would always reunite with our loved ones, even after death. Meanwhile, I was still engulfed in grief, worrying about him. A heavy silence hung between us until I sensed that a question had been brewing in his mind for some time. Just a few feet from the bookstore, he asked:

"Auntie, but who is he really? Is he your boyfriend? Or who is he?"

"Who do you mean?" I replied.

"The one who is always with you, who goes home with you, whom my mum liked so much that was at her funeral and who is always by your side. Who is he?"

"He is the one who accompanies me," I told him.

"As a boyfriend or what?" he pressed.

"I can't say for sure, Esteban. He is my companion."

Still unsatisfied, he continued, "But he goes with you to the United States, Slovakia, and everywhere!"

Fortunately, we arrived at the bookstore just then. As I stepped out, I thought to myself, "This weekend, it is I—far more than he—who needs some psychological work."

Wolfgang is an Austrian architect whom I met for the first time in 2005. One of my cousins had met him in Barcelona where he was on transit after participating in the Venice Biennial. My cousin called me immediately and told me he would like me to meet Wolfgang. Thanks to his insistence, in 2006 I visited the foundation for which Wolfgang worked. It was an old colonial structure of two floors, right in downtown Bogotá. He was in one of the office rooms on the second floor, going through some maps on his computer. I was introduced to him during a tour of the headquarters, and as he turned around, I said to myself, "Indeed, my cousin was right. I really had to meet him." He was tall and slim with deep blue eyes, and a smile that seemed to sparkle at the corner of his lips. I admired his manners, his gentleness, his simplicity, and his openness. We began a conversation about traditional housing in the Pacific, and from there a connection grew.

Day by day, week by week, we spent more time together. We talked endlessly about human dignity. He was working with reintegrated youth in the slums of Bogotá. He was quite obsessed with architecture, a subject he frequently discussed with me, leading me to develop a greater appreciation of structures and spaces, as well as to become more conscious about equality in design. I would say to him that his motto could be summed up as "fair architecture." It was during a long, eight-hour train journey between

Austria and Slovakia that he helped me refine the concept for Visible Hands, the foundation I established after leaving the ministry. From the very first moment, I found in him a strong bond grounded in our mutual causes and personal outlooks: we enjoyed strolling through cities, hiking mountains, and watching the sea.

For eight years, this tall, blond Austrian with fair skin that never reddened in the sun but rather retained an orange hue I so much loved, was the only person, apart from my family, with whom I shared my life in its profundity. He knew everything about me, from my likes and dislikes, my silences and joys, including, as you would imagine, my moments of sorrow. He had a remarkable ability to listen and knew exactly how to calm me. Yet he never intruded into my personal space. We both needed a way of relating that was intimate yet distant, somewhat undefined. Wolfgang was both my anchor and my source of restlessness. In the end, in spite of all we went through and the disruptions, he was my true companion on the journey.

I knew it wasn't easy for Wolfgang to cope with the realities of my ministerial position. He had known me long before this chapter of my life, during a time when we couldn't have imagined what was to come. After my appointment was announced, he kept his distance, and we didn't reconnect for several months—long enough for both of us to adjust to the new circumstances. Wolfgang was simple and discreet, resistant to the rules of hierarchy and the dynamics of power. He was deeply immersed in his own world of structures and ideas. The shift in my life took a toll on him, as it did on all of us. We could no longer go out without being observed, interrupted by greetings, questions, or invitations to sit and chat. Even when he accompanied me to various events, he would often express his desire to share moments with me rather than with others—regardless of their fame or status. That simply didn't matter to him. In truth, our meetings were usually either at my house or in a quiet spot in the countryside, where we could preserve a unique, intimate space for ourselves.

Once, with great enthusiasm, I invited Wolfgang on a two-day tour of the capital cities of the Pacific—something we had always planned to do. However, during that trip, the only real time we shared was on the plane. Upon landing, he seemed to vanish as I became caught up in receptions, greeting local authorities, children, and everyone in between. Each time

I got into the car for another destination, I would ask about Wolfgang, only to be told by one of my escorts that he had gone off with one of my collaborators.

Ultimately, we found ourselves back at the airport to board our return flight. Once on board, we managed to chat for about five minutes before I dozed off, exhausted from the day's intensity. As we landed in Bogotá, he turned to me and said, "This is definitely the last time I'm accompanying you on a tour. I don't even exist on your agenda. It bothers me that we can't spend a moment together because you're always with all these people." On another occasion, he expressed his frustration over my divided attention. "You want to do everything at once: job, family, affection . . . you weigh them all equally. You can't succeed in everything with this level of intensity."

Over time, I realized he was right. Most of the time, I wasn't truly present. I was a workaholic, and by the end of the day, I had little energy left for those around me. Yet despite his complaints, he remained a vital part of my life. He was steadfast in his friendship, loyalty, and discretion. Above all, he provided me with a safe space to share my thoughts without the fear of them being used against me. I knew he wouldn't ask anything of me out of self-interest; I felt assured that he loved me dearly and was deeply committed to our relationship, undefined as it was.

We never really fit into any clear category. "Is it easy to classify all personal relationships?" I used to ask myself. We were two free spirits, unconventional, existing in a space that didn't need a label. Wolfgang occupied a transcendental space in my life that I left undefined. He was always there for me, at midnight or noon, in Austria or Colombia. Esteban, my nephew, was right. Who was he? He did not fit into any definition. It was hard to tell—not even Wolfgang or I could fully answer that question.

Part VI

The Runaway Slave of the Rain

We only harm others when we are unable to imagine them.
—Carlos Fuentes

I was nearing the eighth month of my tenure as minister when I was invited to open the Hay Festival, one of the country's most important international events. As I arrived in Cartagena, I was greeted by a refreshing breeze that contrasted with the sweltering heat. The star of the evening was Baaba Maal, a renowned African singer from Senegal, visiting the city for the first time. He was aware of Cartagena as one of the main ports where thousands of Africans were forcefully disembarked over centuries.

I had the opportunity to meet him before the concert. He was a tall man with a radiant smile, his dark skin framed by a special blue silk robe, with sleeve edges adorned with intricate arabesque embroidery—a garment that conveyed royalty. We exchanged warm hugs that felt like a reunion of ancestral soulmates. As I welcomed him, he was relentless in his curiosity about the Black presence in Cartagena, a sister city to Dakar, and connected to the island of Gorée. His flurry of questions revealed his need to decipher these other parts of Senegal and the broader African continent, which, despite the deep horror and trauma, re-create their existence on the other side of the Atlantic.

Soon it was time to start the show. I joined the first row of the plaza filled with people all dressed in white, the dress code during major elite events in this city. In my mind, I started questioning why, in the heart of the Black, Mestizo, Mulatto, and Arab Caribbean, a place that was everything other than lacking in color and variety, just white was the color of choice. I was the only one not wearing white, simply because I did not know it was the custom. I made space for myself in the crowd and soon moved close to Charles King, a well-known local musician generally referred to as the king of the *champeta*. Champeta is a music genre that resulted from the appropriation of African and Afro-diasporic rhythms such as Congolese *soukous* and Jamaican *ragamuffin* by the inhabitants in the major Black neighborhoods of the city, far away from that historical center.

The stage lights were turned on, emitting dim brightness; meanwhile, as if in a ritual, there emerged from the backstage a *griot* with his *kora*. The show began; we were into a rhythm that took us on a journey to the desert, to the river Niger and the river Senegal, to the Mandinka Empire, that is, present-day Mali, to a place across the Atlantic. Far away as these places were, the mystical power of each kora string brought them nearer and nearer to us. The griot, this sacred and legendary West African poet described by the Nigerian Nobel Laureate Wole Soyinka as "the original poet, the epic narrator and the custodian of history in that region," walked slowly as he struck his kora, a West African calabash harp that they alone know how to play. This moment marked a kind of silent, subtle, and deep interlude that cleared the way for Baaba Maal's voice in his native Pulaar language. He was trailed on stage by a set of musicians, led by the talking drum player, who seemed to initiate the conversation with the lyrics, accompanied by the sound of the kora in the backdrop. The force of the music felt like a rhythmic umbilical cord. From the podium, Baaba Maal greeted the crowd and said, "Good evening, Cartagena. Where are my Black people, my Africa in this place? Let me see your hands, please!" Only Charles and I raised our hands. We were the only two Blacks in the crowd raising our hands (in a city where half of the population, whether or not they identify themselves as such, is of African and Palenque ancestry). The whole place went momentarily silent. The Black Cartagena Baaba Maal was greeting with emotion was not there. Throughout the concert I kept asking myself: How on earth do I explain this to him? How do I tell him that behind these walls live more than one million Blacks who would have euphorically shouted, "Here we are, brother," who would have happily searched his face, trying to find out which of their cousins or uncles looked like him? Without doubt, they would have danced and sang along, given that, both in Africa and here, freedom continues to be a struggle and music a major instrument of liberation.

I knew for sure that the absence of Black people at the concert was no accident. It reflected the reality of a deeply segregated city. Black people, whose ancestors had built those very walls, its landmark feature, still lived on the margins, far from the city's opulence, glamour, and welfare. I wondered if anyone in the audience was questioning this, or if they preferred to ignore this Black Cartagena without public services and the night-time transport system. This other Cartagena was only welcomed to serve rather than to enjoy the historic center. Baaba Maal met me as he stepped down from the podium at the end of the concert and, gazing steadily at me, he exclaimed, "It is difficult here, isn't it?" I could only reply, "In this city we are just decoration and servants. We still need to free ourselves and become full citizens in society. Here, we are still to achieve real independence." To someone like him who had created a movement that used music as a form of political expression of autonomy and dignity, there was no need to explain further. With deep affection, we hugged each other once more, just to say, courage and *A la prochaine*!

"At least I was there. Imagine if he hadn't met any Black people at all?" I felt frustrated to consider the presence of one or two Black people as a sign of victory. Each time I have been back in Cartagena for any event, no matter how beautiful the aesthetic or how spectacular the program seemed, I have no longer felt at ease. After Baaba Maal, other friends of mine such as Susana Baca, Carlinhos Brown, and Seu Jorge, just to mention a few, asked me the same question: Paula, where are the Black people here? Why is it just you? And someone like Carlinhos even went a step further to invite the key champeta musicians to his rehearsal, concert, and, as a first in the history of the festival, he called them up to the podium. The day after the festival, Susana was able to get a means of transport to take her to Palenque de San Basilio, the first bastion of Black freedom and a world heritage site a two-hour drive from Cartagena. There, everything breathes of Africanness. In the middle of his stage performance, Seu Jorge, on his part, recited "Negro Drama," a song by the great rapper and favela poet Racionais Mc's. At the end, each of these musicians, as renowned as they are, found their own answers. They have suffered the same problems in their countries. We were all exceptional cases in societies segregated not by law but by a lack of will to advance equal opportunities for Afro-descendent communities. It was not a coincidence that the map of poverty and violence corresponded to areas occupied mainly by our communities.

I was no stranger to the experience of exclusion in that city, even as a Black woman in a position of power at that time. At the top hotels, I saw how everyone was allowed entry without any form of scrutiny, while I was stopped and asked where I was going and why. Once I was relaxing, having a drink in a public square with a group of Black women. A group of men approached us on the presumption that we were sex workers. Another time, in one of Cartagena's finest hotels, someone in the elevator asked me if I was a masseuse or what kind of service I was offering. This did not just happen in Cartagena or on special events; it was a matter of everyday life. Even as a minister, I was often met with disbelief when I introduced myself, with people insisting, "Please, call for the minister." The scene at the concert repeated itself over and over and in most situations. The only one to say, "Even if what you see is just me or a handful of us, we are millions who belong to this nation."

Chapter 20

She Is Black, But . . .

With a packed schedule of countless events to attend, I began to notice certain patterns that left me on edge. Hosts would welcome me warmly, only to follow up with comments like, "I like Black people," "Afro people are so happy," "The gardener and the domestic worker at home are Black; that's why Afro people are so close to my heart," or "At my golf club, I have a Black caddy that I'm so fond of." They would even ask, "How can I interact with people like you?" or "Why aren't all the Black people in this country united under a single agenda?" It was exhausting, to say the least, and often quite depressing, especially since these comments would come out of nowhere as soon as I said hello, without me prompting any questions or reflections.

On one occasion, fed up with such conversations, I decided to confront a woman who had been particularly patronizing. I asked her how it would sound if I expressed my fondness for Whites and Mestizos, generalized about White people, or questioned why White or Mestizo individuals weren't united. I wanted to know why she felt the need to justify or validate herself in this way. For me, this topic was closed. Once a government official asked me:

> "Paula, tell me, do you honestly think there is discrimination in Colombia?"
>
> "Yes, of course," I answered.
>
> "Hold on, Paula, how dare you say that?" he replied. "Look, my former housemaids are Black and I treated them with the same affection as members of my family. I even bought a home for them."

Listening to him, what went through my mind was: why should I congratulate you for being a fair employer and for appreciating someone's service in the upkeep of your family?

Whenever I visited an institution, my host would immediately introduce me to their Black employees or colleagues, usually one or two, as if to showcase how liberal and progressive they were. I couldn't help but wonder why the diversity of their workforce was perceived as something exceptional. Several questions flooded my mind: Why did I have to congratulate them for the obvious? For whom were they doing a favor? Weren't we citizens with talents like anyone else? Once, I questioned a business leader about why there were only one or two Black CEOs or individuals in top management positions among the hundred largest enterprises in Colombia. He gave a shocking response: "Paula, if people like you are good at sports, isn't it better to develop your talent in that area?" I couldn't believe what I was hearing. Yes, we excel in sports, but our talents extend far beyond that. It seemed that our skills and contributions were invisible to them. I began to try to understand their perspective, wondering if this was a way of acknowledging their guilt and recognizing that something was fundamentally wrong with their mindset.

Still, on another occasion, a journalist asked me, "Why do you people become so fierce when referred to as people of color, dark-skinned, Negro, or Black, even when it is said with affection? How do you want us to call you, then?" I began by questioning his use of "you people," explaining that it implied we were an entity apart from the rest of the population, almost like an unknown species. I emphasized that it wasn't a matter of "you" versus "us," but rather "we"—we Colombians. I pressed further: "How would you feel if, after barely knowing each other, I greeted you with, 'Hi White, hi Mestizo'? Would you be comfortable with that? How would you prefer to be called?" He replied, "I want to be called by my first name." I told him it was the same for me and for anyone from a minority group considered different. In our intimate and close relationships, we can decide the way we want to be called, but it is uncomfortable for someone you do not know to label you in a way that might not resonate with your experience. On another occasion, someone asked, "Why do you people refer to yourselves as Afro-descendants? I prefer calling you Blacks. How would it sound if I defined myself as Ibero-descendant? Doesn't that seem incoherent?" I explained that the term "Afro-descendant" carries a legacy of liberation stemming from one of the greatest forms of oppression in human history, and that claiming this legacy meant a lot to me. After all, every identity group has the right to define how it wishes to be identified. Were we as Afro descendants excluded from this right?

In another forum, I was asked, "Does it then mean that you are 'Afro privileged?" I told the journalist, "Why is attending a good university and having access to certain opportunities considered 'normal' to others but become a matter of privilege in our case?" I did not want to create this category. Equal access to opportunities should be something normal for anyone, irrespective of their skin color. He replied, "Yes, the thing is that you are Black, but . . . with your profile, it is not normal." I did not get it. Why the *but*? Does being Black imply certain limitations when it comes to the quality of education or opportunities? Even if the gap in the access to opportunities was evident, we were not supposed to state it as if it were an unchangeable reality. She fell silent.

At times, even within my team and working groups in the government, it seemed like requesting actions related to Afro issues was seen as a personal favor. Some individuals even overlooked the fact that I was Black. They would say things like, "The thing is, you are different. . . . Afro communities can be so difficult." One colleague even confided, "Paula, I personally do not like Indigenous people." I widened my eyes and replied, "So you don't like Blacks either; we're in the same boat."

One of the frequent questions that I had to answer during my trips abroad was whether there were Black people in Colombia. For example, a Colombian expatriate said to me, "But in Colombia there are hardly any Black people; you are mistaken, minister." All I said was, "Just take a look at the Colombian national football team, for instance." It pained me to note the way Colombians living abroad would erase or downplay the presence of Black people in Colombia, as if to suggest that our country was nothing but White, or if anything, Mestizo. For some of them, Black presence was only convenient and welcomed as far as sports were concerned. It never crossed their mind that we were the third country in the Americas and outside Africa with the highest Afro-descendant population, nor did they consider such a transnational identity as a strength or asset. It was even more surprising to me that these same people faced discrimination abroad for being Latinos. In the end, one can say that the consequences of colonialism are still prevalent. As the Kenyan intellectual Ngugi wa Thiong'o explains in his book *Decolonising the Mind* (1986):

> The effect of a cultural bomb is to annihilate a people's belief in their names, in their languages, in their environment, in their heritage of struggle, in their unity, in their capacities and ultimately in themselves. It makes them see their past as one wasteland of non-achievement and it makes them want to distance themselves from that wasteland.

As time went on, I realized there was a profound ignorance surrounding the subject of ethnicity, which often compelled me to adopt a pedagogical attitude despite my nature. Although I had never considered myself particularly diplomatic, I decided to give it a try. Taking on the role of a teacher, I resolved to use examples to illustrate my point. Whenever someone asked me where I was born, I would respond, "Bogotá." Automatically, they would reply, "Weren't you born in Chocó?" I would clarify, "No." Their expressions were often filled with astonishment and surprise. I then explained that as human beings, we can be born anywhere and live in any part of the world, can't we?

My attitude may have come across as aggressive in response to comments intended as compliments. However, one of the many lessons I learned during that time is that, when faced with certain situations and individuals, it is essential to be clear and categorical while still showing respect. I was often astonished by how some people lacked the humility to admit their limited knowledge about ethnic issues. The dynamics of exclusion and discrimination are deeply embedded in the collective unconscious that the majority is raised within. Confronting these issues requires profound reflection and a continuous awakening to expose the prejudice, undervaluation, and, at times, contempt that lie beneath the surface.

The recognition we seek goes beyond physical and cultural traits or the epithets of our identity. I do not mean to imply that everyone needs to know everything about every ethnic group, but there are basic standards of respect that should be upheld.

Chapter 21

The Color of the Invisible

In many interactions, I found that the color of my skin rendered me invisible in ways that were both subtle and overt. This invisibility often manifested in comments that dismissed or minimized my experiences and those of ethnic communities. For instance, when I raised issues related to racial equity, I was sometimes met with indifference. The underlying message was clear: the struggles of Black individuals were often overlooked, relegated to the margins of broader societal discussions, often viewed through an American lens even though the Colombian experience differs significantly.

During meetings, I could sense a disconnect; my colleagues would nod along, yet their expressions reflected a lack of understanding of the complexities surrounding race. It was as if they were engaging with a concept rather than with a person who had lived these experiences. This dynamic not only silenced my voice but also perpetuated a cycle of invisibility that many in the Afro-descendant community face daily. I often found myself questioning how we could make the invisible visible. How could we bridge the gap between rhetorical acknowledgment and effective action? These questions would stay with me, shaping my path in the next chapter of my life.

Over time, people began to realize and ask themselves: What is the acceptable number of Whites, Indigenous people, Blacks, men, or women in a given space? Is there an ideal quota? Once I was asked to recommend a Black person for an award, and when I submitted a list, I was told, "Paula, we don't have enough space for that many Blacks. Just one for now, and maybe another in a year or two." They often remarked that they didn't want the space to feel "too Black."

Soon after, I started receiving more calls, turning me into a de facto agency for Afro talents. Many began to seek more diversity but expected me to handle it for them. I was willing to help pave the way for others, yet I realized this was also a convenient way for them to avoid actively searching for diverse talent. They assumed I knew all the Black leaders in the country and to do the work for free, all while claiming their doors were open but there were not competent Black candidates. Thus, on top of my substantial responsibilities, I found myself functioning as a self-funded headhunter. Over time, I realized how unfair this was.

There was no doubt that if the majority in a space were White or Mestizo, it wouldn't raise any eyebrows. I began grappling with concepts like "equal but not equal" and "participation is fine, but just a little." It felt more like a gesture than a genuine commitment, as if too many Black people might "invade" it. This was a rather violent attitude. In many contexts, quotas became necessary because many were unwilling to share power through mere persuasion or ethics. They remained entrenched in the belief that one Black individual was enough.

Even in cooperation agencies or programs aimed at supporting Afro-Colombians, it became normalized to work for us without us for many years. They failed to see the incoherence in this approach and the critical need for Black professionals to be part of their teams. The prevailing philosophy seemed to be, "We are helping you; we know how to make you better." This invisibility—being treated as objects of intervention rather than as subjects with agency—was what confronted me the most. It highlighted the need for diverse perspectives to contribute to the advancement of the entire country.

In those moments, I was involved in a thorough soul searching, wondering if I was becoming paranoid. I asked myself if so much explanation, so much justification, so much confrontation was, after all, due to my character. I was losing so much time and energy having to tackle this issue every now and then. Did this deserve to be the highlight of my agenda as minister and the rest of my life? Did I deserve to keep deconstructing discourses and practices, and going this extra mile, only to end up saying, "Hey guys, we are here, so let us try to be equal?" Honestly speaking, given my level of exposure, this issue became unsettling to me as the days went by. It made me feel like an exotic element, a token, or a joker. So what was

I supposed to do? The first thing was to acknowledge that, beyond the anecdotes, we lived in a deeply sick and racist society. My choice was not to get used to it, but neither was I going to quarrel about it all the time. I needed to choose my battles wisely for the sake of my emotional, mental, and physical health.

I chose to focus on what I could achieve through my ministerial position, even if it meant facing rejection. For instance, I initiated a yearly commemoration of the work of our greatest Colombian writers from various eras. We developed a rich agenda with partners to honor the literary memory and legacy of the country. However, when the time came to commemorate the works of two great Afro-Colombian poets from the Caribbean coast, Candelario Obeso and Jorge Artel, some key institutions that had supported previous initiatives suddenly withdrew. I reached out to insist on their support, but they simply replied that they did not agree with giving such recognition to these writers. One of the country's most well-known journalists even told me that Candelario Obeso—our own version of Nicolás Guillén or Aimé Césaire—was a resentful character. I spent nearly an hour explaining Obeso´s significance, how his poetry was an expression of his pain and frustration in nineteenth-century Colombia, as someone moving from a period of slavery to that of rhetorical freedom. He was a polyglot and highly erudite figure. I repeated off-hand my favorite poem by the author, a poem about solidarity, despite the categories and spatial demarcations imposed by human society.

For every initiative related to ethnicity, it felt like we were pioneers, breaking new ground. We organized the first exhibition at the National Museum focused on Afro-Colombians in the Caribbean and Indigenous peoples in the Amazon. We launched traditional music programs, highlighting the Marimba and chirimía routes. I was convinced that these initiatives would resonate deeply, even if only symbolically, reflecting the collective yearning of our national consciousness. But often I found myself pushing the long-standing team to confront whose cultures were left out or behind in our public actions, whose Colombians were not part of our priorities.

One notable example was the Bicentennial commemoration. Our main priority was to project the country's forgotten memories. We created a collection of Afro-Colombian and Indigenous writers, a comprehensive compilation of the best literary works by Black and Indigenous authors, many of which were unpublished and thus unknown to the general public. We convened a high-profile editorial committee with the support of various universities, resulting in the publication of thousands of copies that were distributed to public libraries and cultural centers, becoming critical reference sources. But then a major scandal emerged concerning the Afro-Colombian literary collection, a mini library with more than twenty books. The main cultural magazine of Bogotá ran an article titled "The Presence of the Invisible." The author questioned the collection through the following arguments: "Why such an investment of State resources in this collection? Will it make the invisible visible? No doubt, it sounds good and powerful, such as something supernatural, magical or with sorcery." The entire content of the piece was rather offensive in nature. The author misrepresented the fact that my name was mentioned in the acknowledgments section of the collection. I asked myself: when the names of other ministers and public officials featured in similar endeavors, was that also considered as proselytism? In my case, it was frowned at as something suspicious and even as political maneuvering. The article claimed that referring to "invisibility" was a gross exaggeration. Beneath these criticisms lay a sense of contempt and disrespect, particularly because we had published works by more than thirty Afro-Colombian authors. However, the most significant response came from our literary team at the ministry and a network of scholars from various parts of the world. Thanks to their efforts, the news outlet and its contributor retracted their statements just a few days later.

The real question was: Why did this issue spark such controversy? There are many possible answers, from the discomfort caused by addressing epistemic justice to the resistance against recognizing ethnic cultural heritage. Researcher Claudia Mosquera delved into these dynamics, analyzing the cultural and conceptual exclusions embedded in the "you" and "us" discourses that became central to this debate.

> The author constructs a locus of enunciation, a "we" which includes them and which is made up of white-mestizo Euro-descendant subjects, heirs to western reason, the real Colombians, integrated into the nation, custodians of national culture. Opposed to this "we", the author creates out of the blue a certain "they" that corresponds to the

> Afro-Colombians, rhetorical subjects, invisibilized and obscure victims in need of bureaucratic reflectors; pseudo-invisibilized subjects who reproduce hierarchies within the ambits of invisibility, ignoring the challenges posed in today's society by national cultural hegemony.

The first to respond to the controversy were academics, activists, and the ministerial literary team. It was not about me or the columnist; it was about recognizing the power of culture in advancing racial equity in Colombia. Lack of access to intellectual production of Afro-Colombian writers perpetuates a single, almost colorless national narrative. Different geographies, hopes, frustrations, and moments make these writings a veritable politics of liberation not only for their authors but also for their readers, interpreters, and those who continue to rewrite them today. Untold stories turn out to be a curse to memory and continue to foment the permanently partial narratives of a nation still in the quest for its sites of meaning. A good proportion of the violence stems from the series of systematic omissions, many of them symbolic in nature, which dehumanize every now and then a sizable segment of our population. Our national narrative was constructed on a foundation that omits an Indigenous, Black, peasant, feminine nation with great regional strength and autonomy. It has been a history written more with an eraser than with a pencil.

The main allusion to Black population among average Colombians is slavery with a poor understanding of its abolition—abolition as a concession by the slave masters, ignoring the efforts of the enslaved Africans. This standpoint of the slave master, the colonizer, and modern developmentalist approaches has often built on the discourse of the noble savage in need of civilization. This literary collection was crucial, given the magnitude of the task ahead, as we needed to keep focus on other forms of cultural exclusions begging to be addressed such as cinema, theater, and painting, just to name a few. Music genres such as cumbia and bullerengue have always expressed an insistent cry for freedom and against injustice, with the "why" recurring in the chorus, "why do you hit me?" "why, why, why?" More recently, such has been the case in hip-hop, with groups such as Chocquibtown addressing the issue head-on in their songs like "where I come from" and the chorus "everybody has, everybody goes . . . except us."

I witnessed the transformation of Paula who, at the beginning of her tenure as minister, was afraid to share her views for the fear of the reactions they might provoke—not only because of potential backlash but also because she felt she lacked the necessary arguments and experiences to respond confidently. Simply being a Black woman was not enough to fully grasp and lead a racial struggle, as skin color is tied to a deeply subjective experience, beneath which lies a profound ethical question.

By assuming my tenure at twenty-eight-years-old, I was just a young, Black, Bogotá-born, middle-class woman, half shielded by the economic and psychological conditions paved for her by her mother and her aunts. My understanding of the racial struggle was incomplete. For me, the ministry became both a school and a laboratory. As the days went by, I grappled with distinguishing between what was due to ignorance and what was part of a deliberate, calculated, and harmful system. One cannot deny identity politics. Some people have vested interests in making sure that racism persists and even thrives. The mechanisms of racism can be subtle at times and, at others, blatantly obvious. Over time, I started adopting a more balanced and constructive approach, avoiding generalizations about people's experiences and intentions. However, I was not in a position of power and privilege to remain silent.

Sometimes everything seemed to me so *primitive*, so basic, to be more precise. I had assumed that others had already fought the battles for me and that the struggle was nearly over, but I was wrong. While many past leaders had treated the infection in one area, I realized that new infections were still spreading. The venom was still alive, and I had my own role to play in the ongoing struggle, not as a hero but as a part of a collective and permanent effort of committed individuals. Even though at times I felt fire burning in my bones, I understood I needed more patience, love, and also more pragmatism. The emotional draining was enormous, and it was not good for me. Maintaining my emotional balance was essential to building bridges and not walls. Hence, I learned to approach challenges with greater analysis, while holding onto passion and hope, always guided by love. The truth is, I became less naive and innocent, but stronger, fully aware that I was not alone in this fight.

What gave me strength was the memory of my ancestral lineage—the memory of these African women who, amid oppression, used the art of hair braiding to map out their escape routes. Even when I felt daunted and demoralized, the spirit of resilience flowed through my African veins. I did not lose sight of the fact that two or three generations down the line, my ancestors could not, in their wildest dreams, imagine I would be here, sharing my experiences in this book. That means we are bound to forge ahead like those runaway slaves who, come rain come shine, found their freedom. The time will come for us, not just to remain in a constant state of resistance but one of joy and fulfillment to create a space for a new ethical revolution.

Part VII

"Goodbye, Minister"

"Goodbye, minister, goodbye, minister . . . minister, goodbye." Toward the end of 2009, that was the song on the lips of Ines Granja, a cultural figure from the Colombian Pacific coast. It was an adaptation of her song "Adios Margarita" (Goodbye Margarita). Granja welcomed me at the shores of the Río Timbiquí with fireworks as I arrived in a motorboat, having navigated the vastness of the Pacific Ocean for an hour before entering one of its tributaries, accompanied by a group of ambassadors and media representatives. We were there to attend the closing of two Ministry initiatives: one focused on women's networks and cultural preservation, and the other on the Marimba Route, which supports traditional music schools. I wanted to ensure these initiatives received the backing of the international community, especially as I prepared to step down from my role as minister, while also highlighting their immense value to the Colombian public.

Timbiquí is a Black Macondo lost in the jungle, a place rich in minerals, music dynasties, and breathtaking rivers and seas, interspersed with estuaries and mangroves, all filled with unique stories. Mauro Castillo, the storyteller and chronicler of Timbiquí, reflects on the history of these musical dynasties, specifically the Balanta family: "If Gabriel García Márquez had not been born in Aracataca but in Timbiquí, the Buendía family would have been the Balanta." This dynasty of musicians and singers traces its lineage back to ancient Africa, specifically to the Balanta ethnic group from Guinea-Bissau and southern Senegal, in the Casamance region. We had the honor of participating in a concert featuring these music schools, directed by members of these dynasties, and enjoyed a gastronomic festival and market organized by local women.

This event allowed us to taste the food and traditional beverages that are true hallmarks of the country.

In Timbiquí, the group of women involved in the Ministry's program were carriers of intertwined life stories, filled with struggles, joyful laments, and profound wisdom. Through their songs, they transformed their experiences, mourning the past while embracing hope for the future. As one young singer from the Pacific said, "We must believe in what we sing, value what we possess, and lovingly embrace and transmit our traditions." These women were guardians, teachers, mothers, psychologists, caregivers, and healers—the invisible protagonists of that magical, mythical, and complex Pacific. In this vibrant network, activities like singing, cooking, fishing, and crafting came together, creating a rich tapestry of cultural expression that was inseparable from the region's identity. The concert we attended, along with the gastronomic festival organized by these women, showcased not only their talents but also the deep connections between their traditions and daily lives. As we celebrated the rich cultural heritage of Timbiquí, I was reminded of an African proverb: "If women lower their arms, the sky will fall." Their courage and commitment to preserving their traditions and fostering their community left an indelible mark on my heart, reinforcing the vital role of women in shaping the future of the Pacific.

The day before our arrival, the guerilla forces had sown terror in that small municipality. Timbiquí was no more the romantic and idyllic place that I had visited a few years earlier. Our visit was unwelcome by criminal groups controlling its waters and mountains through illegal mining and coca cultivation. The river that had so impressed me three years before had lost its emerald green and olive color. Now it looked brownish, a result of mineral exploitation. Its waters were muddy and the ambience tense. But there remained the same men and women, peasant, Black, and smiling, whom I so admired, facing all kinds of threats in their ancestral territory.

I had begun my tenure as minister in Buenaventura, in the Pacific, and now here I was again, in Timbiquí, still in the Pacific, as I neared the end of one of the most decisive periods of my life. This visit reaffirmed my conviction that we were united in the struggle, that the marimbas and chants would continue to nurture our determination to live in defiance of fear and atrocity. Resisting and existing in the face of unending threats has never been an easy task. As I bid farewell as minister, I reflected on how these communities would forever be woven into the fabric of my life, shaping my future in ways I had yet to fully understand. Their resilience and spirit would accompany me as I returned to a new chapter, one that honored the connections forged during my time in service.

Chapter 22

My Kindred Soul

Though I shared the holidays with ten cousins, my bond with two of them, Patricia and Raúl, was particularly special. Patricia, daughter of my aunt Carmen, was my kindred soul and one of the strongest pillars of my life. She was my sister and my buddy. Even if we fell out over an issue and exchanged bitter words, love always resolved everything. I could say that in the same way that my aunt Cecilia helped to raise me during holidays, and my aunt Carmen helped to shape my dreams, Patricia was just as important for the rest of my life.

My cousin was born in 1969 and passed away unexpectedly in 2012. In my childhood, she would take care of me and pick me up from school when my mother was at work. I recall how she offered me Coca-Cola in the place of baby milk. Fortunately, I survived. Patricia was my model of a woman and a professional. She was a focused and resolute character, like most of the women in my family, but at the same time she had this rare sense of caustic and biting humor. She was obsessed with tidiness (her hobby was ironing clothes!), was a tireless worker, and an exemplary mother. I remained very close to her children while she was busy pursuing her career.

I was twelve when Patricia began her studies at university, concentrating in psychology. As a psychologist, she specialized in child abuse cases and learning difficulties. Patricia was unwavering in her belief that society must acknowledge child abuse and provide systematic support for its victims. In 2010, alongside two partners, we founded Visible Hands, and during the final years of her life, she poured her heart into laying a solid foundation for this shared dream. She played an active role in selecting and training the first cohort of Visible Hands in Cartagena, Cali, and Medellín.

In 2012, at the age of forty-two, Patricia died unexpectedly from a genetic cardiac condition. One fateful Sunday, toward the end of July, my phone rang at 7 a.m. When I picked up, it was Patricia, sounding very restless. She told me she was feeling terrible, experiencing acute chest pain, and was getting ready to go to the clinic. I jumped out of bed, hailed a taxi, and immediately called my mother, and together we rushed Patricia to the hospital.

Before entering the operating room, she managed to thank us several times, expressing how much we meant to her. Turning to me, she repeatedly said, "My kids, my kids, Paulita." Her last gaze held a blend of deep love and strength, as if she sensed what was about to happen. Still, she remained defiant, poised to face whatever came next, just as she always had. All I could see was the stretcher moving past the green-painted doors of the operating room.

Even in that desperate moment, it never crossed my mind that it would be the last time I would see and talk to Patricia. She was my right hand, my left hand, the other half of my brain, and the other half of my heart. Until then I had always rationalized that death was part of life. But in that moment, I was engulfed by an internal tremor, resisting any attempt by my reasoning to accept the reality of Patricia's departure. I wept uncontrollably, unable to think of anything else, gripped by a profound sense of emptiness that deepened with each passing day. Eventually, I found the strength to write the following tribute for her funeral.

> Farewell to Patricia Álvarez, July 29, 2012
> I loved Patricia with all my heart. Even if we were bonded by blood ties by virtue of being cousins, life, our shared experiences, and the deep respect we had for each other made her my sister, my confidante, my psychotherapist, my buddy, my editor, and, simply, my best friend. She infected me and filled my life with her characteristic affection and sense of total commitment; even when I wasn't an easy character, I don't remember her ever reproaching me. She would remain part and parcel of the defining dreams of my life. I loved Patricia with all my heart, and I am grateful to God for every single second I spent with her. I asked God to let Patricia be with me for a little more time, pleading with Him to let me enjoy her presence for just one more time . . . I will dearly miss her. . . . It was always clear to us that we were each other's keeper, sister, kindred soul. But she has left me and the only thing I ask from God is that, wherever He has preserved

> her soul, let her experience happiness, fullness, and freedom and that her closeness to us should remain, in whatever form, long-lasting.
>
> Patty, you were fond of reading my speeches before I delivered them, offering your comments and correcting them so that the final version reflected our sense of love, mission, and calling. Henceforth, you won't read them anymore. Well, there comes a moment when, just like in other aspects of life, I need to thrive on my own, to prove what I learned from you. That is the only way I can repay an everlasting homage to your presence in my life.

I shall never forget one of the moments we spent together during my time as minister. Although we couldn't meet and share as often as we'd like, we always found ways to make up for those absences. One memorable occasion, I called Patricia to tell her I had secured front-row tickets to see her favorite artist, Miguel Bosé (a top Spanish singer). On the day of the concert, we arrived early and settled into our seats just two or three yards from where Miguel Bosé would appear. As the concert began, we screamed with excitement. In those moments, I transformed completely; at concerts or salsa performances, I was unstoppable. Patricia looked at me, amused, and said, "Is this child possessed or what?" That night, we had the time of our lives—she even more than I. We became oblivious to everything else, as if the world outside vanished, leaving only Miguel and us.

When Miguel Bosé made his appearance on stage, singing "I shall be the wind that blows," we joined in with the chorus, "You won't say no, you won't say no." As he continued with "I will be your outlaw lover, outlaw," the frenzy in the crowd reached a peak, and we shouted back, "heart, heart, broken heart." At the end of the song, we all sang together, "I will be your loving hero, I will be your hero." Then, he took us down memory lane with "Querida" (Sweetheart). This time, we didn't sing; instead, we howled along, "queriiiiida (sweeeeetie), queriiiiida, (sweeeeetie)." When he performed "My Dark-Skinned Woman," we nodded our heads in rhythm, echoing the ending of the song with "well, well, well, well . . . coffee."

Those moments of joy were just a part of our shared experiences. It was always fun for us to watch a horror film—one of Patricia's favorites—or indulge in our beloved food ritual of Chocóramo cake with peach yogurt. I miss so many things about her, like watching her savor her afternoon dose of cigarettes or relish a sweet treat during tough times. Leaning against a window frame, she would let the smoke swirl out, gazing pensively into the horizon as if seeking metaphysical answers to the issues we were analyzing together.

I miss the way she would tease me when a catchy song got stuck in my head, singing it fifty times a day. In those moments, she'd say, "Forget it . . . it's nice, but come on." I even miss how she would pull my cheeks, pinching them playfully and calling out my middle name, "Marcelitaaaaa." It was her way of stopping me in my tracks whenever I seemed weary or strained.

I will miss her boots, which she rarely took off, relishing the added height that made her feel sleek and confident. The force of her high heels announced her presence with every assertive step, declaring, "Here I am!" After Patricia passed away, my life felt like a table without an axis, leaving me unsteady and poised to fall. I had no choice but to navigate this imbalance.

Yet today, I find solace in the understanding that there are other axes—sisters and affections—that partially fill the void she left behind. Time, the master teacher, reveals the freedom of love. As contradictory and disconcerting as death can be, it reminds us to embrace life more fully, making us more alive and present in each moment.

Chapter 23

"She Does Not Know When to Call It Quits"

"She does not know how to hold herself back," my cousin and sister Patricia would repeat to her children whenever she was talking about me. Even if she found me almost perfect, she never failed to remind me that my major flaw was not knowing when to take a break or when to call it quits. She felt that I was always driven by eagerness and was obsessed with everything. She cared so much about my health because she desperately wanted to see me thrive and to make sure I was not lonely. That is why, as much as we could, we would chat for long hours, especially in the evening and more so on weekends, whenever I visited her at her home and she prepared my favorite dishes. Then she would say to her kids, as she seasoned her cuisine, "Your aunt Paulita is eager about everything and is so obsessed with her work that I'm afraid that she'll get sick at any moment. The thing is that she does not notice when she has to call it quits."

In the year 2008, shortly before my thirtieth birthday, I began experiencing heart palpitations that sometimes compelled me, if ever I was on a walk, to pause and take a seat to calm myself. The cardiologist diagnosed me with cardiac arrhythmia and the main recommendation was, "Paula, you need to slow down the rhythm of work and keep calm for a while; if not, you run the risk of a cardiac arrest. No doubt you are still young, but that does not mean you should break yourself." What astonished me the most was the fact that even at night, when asleep, I could perceive the agitated nature of my heartbeat. The cardiologist needed to monitor my cardiac frequency for some days using a Holter monitor, a system that measures cardiac activity through a series of electrodes attached to my chest. After analyzing the results, the doctor asked me what I had done in the afternoon that day, and my response was, "I went to the Ministerial Council and also held some meetings at the Presidency." He drew my attention to the diagram and made it clear to me that it was specifically at such times of the day were the moments of the highest peak. With the help of certain medications and with a growing level of self-care, I started regulating my system. That was the first sign that I was going overboard, just as Patricia had rightly forewarned.

In 2009, I was dealing with another health issue. I went in for a general medical check-up, and the doctor found some fibroids in my body and told me that, due to their size, I needed to consult a specialist immediately. After thorough examination, the specialist told me, "Paula, we have to remove these fibroids as soon as possible. No time to waste. Get ready to be hospitalized. You will be out of the office for at least a month." This warning took a heavy toll on me. In the space of a day, I put my things together, informed the president about the situation and the following day I was already set for the surgery, bidding farewell to my family as if it was my last day. It was a tense and painful moment in my life. I knew all that was happening to me was the result of so much pressure and anxiety, of so many ups and downs, of simply working too much. I always considered myself as a very healthy woman, and I had always been, by God's grace. It was my first time undergoing surgery, and for someone like me who had always strongly believed in the fragility of life, I couldn't shake the fear that it might already be too late to turn back time. When I woke up after the process, I embraced my mum and Raúl who, with Patricia, had accompanied me during the entire operation and recovery period. Fortunately, they succeeded in extracting the fibroids without affecting any of my organs and the biopsy proved that the lumps were benign.

During that brief time in the hospital, I felt utterly helpless, unable to move. Little by little, I was learning the lesson of patience as I waited for my body to regain its strength. It was the right time to start detaching myself from the ministry. Lying there, I realized that everything carried on as usual—nothing came to a halt because of my absence. This experience made me conscious of the fact that I had a life beyond my official duties. I did not receive a single call from anyone in the government, except from the Minister of Social Protection, with whom I had always shared a special rapport. He remained steadfast, taking on my responsibilities during my medical leave. While I appreciated his support, it hurt that no one else reached out to offer a word of encouragement.

Life never ceases to dot our paths with unexpected moments. The director of a media house, Yamid Amat, gave me a call to request an interview. I told him what had happened and the very same day I received an exquisite bouquet of flowers at my house, accompanied by a message so sincere that it has remained forever engraved in my memory.

During my recovery period, I received a visit from five mamos—the highest spiritual Indigenous authorities from the Sierra Nevada in Santa Marta, a natural sanctuary in the Colombian Caribbean. I had visited them several times before, sitting together in total silence by the river, where we raised our thoughts and called on nature spirits for my protection. They tied three threads around my wrists, instructing me not to loosen them until they fell off on their own. These threads were meant to safeguard me and ensure my well-being.

When the mamos came to Bogotá and visited the ministry, they sought me out themselves. Upon learning that I was on medical leave, they asked for my apartment's address and made their way to my home. As I opened the door, I was greeted by five spiritual leaders in their immaculate white garments, accompanied by one of the ministry's advisers. With sheer solemnity, they said, "We learned of your illness and have come to visit you. . . . We can see there is nothing to worry about. It shall be well with you." I offered them seats, and after nearly two hours of conversation about life, one of them asked, "Paula, we would like to see your protection." I realized that only two of the three threads tied to my wrists years before had survived. They took out their skein and tied two more, emphasizing, "It shall be well with you, rest assured." After embracing me, they left, and I was deeply touched by the solidarity and gentleness of that encounter. I felt fulfilled by their presence and their genuine concern for my well-being. This is why I remain deeply connected to these communities; they remind me that, yesterday, today, and tomorrow, I exist first and foremost as a human being.

Chapter 24

The Palenques

In early January 2010, I began planning and organizing my final six months as minister. On the twenty-second of that month, I embarked on a much-needed two-week holiday trip to Providencia, a small Colombian island on the Caribbean coast, renowned for its breathtaking sea of seven colors. I went to the beach, seeking solace in the waves, hoping the sea would carry away all the sad, humiliating, and bitter pages of my life. This ritual was meant to grant me peace, allowing me to let go of old resentments and forgive myself for the many mistakes I had made.

That is how I found myself alone on that tiny island, staying in a charming wooden house, swaying in a hammock and gazing out at the distant sea. During the day, I joined the fishermen, diving into the open waters. They would let me leap from the side of their boats, allowing me to sink and experience the ocean's depth, its beauty and strength enveloping me. Yet I also felt a rush of fear in those dark blue waters when the waves carried me too far from the boat. The fishermen would laugh as I emerged, startled, after a few seconds underwater. They reassured me, saying, "Don't be afraid; nothing is going to happen to you."

In the evenings, I would venture to a different beach, seeking out a Rastafarian bar nestled in a wooden arbor, where reggae music filled the air. I arrived barefoot, dressed however I pleased, ready to enjoy a Coco Loco cocktail prepared just for me. Then I would step out to dance alone, embracing the simplicity of the moment. Here I was free to be myself—unconcerned about appearances, without anyone watching or questions to answer. I would pause occasionally to sing the chorus of one of my favorite Bob Marley songs, letting the music wash over me. There I was, surrendering to the melody of reggae, closing my eyes in a place where, as Bob Marley says in his song "Runaway," I could not escape from my own self. This experience helped me process everything I had gone through. It was time to enjoy myself and leave behind all the fears for the remaining six months ahead of me. The sea provided the peace I needed to prepare for my farewell and to contemplate the kind of Paula I wanted to be after my tenure as minister.

As my term came to a close, I prioritized closing activities, including the Bicentenary celebrations and the Ibero-American Congress of Culture focused on music, while also taking stock of what had been achieved over the past three-and-a-half years. The Ibero-American Congress on Music took place in Medellín in June 2010, marking my first grand farewell ceremony. A month later, we organized the Independence Concert in Quibdó, the capital of Chocó, featuring Juanes. This event ran parallel to more than twelve hundred concerts held across various municipalities, uniting more than two hundred fifty thousand artists for the third edition of the Grand National Concert.

The Ibero-American Congress on Music was an impressive mobilization, uniting many emblematic musicians, music teachers, producers, and ministers from various countries in one space. The entire city of Medellín transformed into a vast stage for an entire week. I dare say it was the event I enjoyed most during my time as minister. My farewell gift was the realization of a dream from my youth: spending time with Silvio Rodríguez, one of the living legends of *nueva trova cubana*. In the days leading up to his concert, we explored the city together, engaging in long conversations and selecting his repertoire of my favorite songs. I joined him in singing my favorite, "Pequeña Serenata Diurna" (Little Daytime Serenade), with its poignant chorus: "I am happy, I am a happy man, and I want the dead ones of my happiness to forgive me for this day." This song perfectly encapsulated my feelings at that moment. The following day, I was captivated by the dedication song "Negra Presuntuosa" (Presumptuous Black Woman), a hymn of Black Peruvian folk music, delivered in the ever-spiritual voice of our great diva, Susana Baca. The song felt like a balm in Gilead, healing the very depths of my being. And of course, there was rumba on the playlist, featuring the Cuban band Los Van Van. Their leader, Juan Formell, kept asking me, "Pauli, what do you want us to play and until what time?" All I could do was to go on enjoying everything in a week that was all music.

That night, I went to bed at dawn, sinking into a king-size bed that felt larger each night, almost as if I were drowning in its vastness. But then, at six in the morning, my phone rang, almost synchronously with the alarm I had set. I was scheduled to visit Son Bata, a group of young Black youths from the Pacific who had participated in LASO, a program designed to promote urban musical genres. These youths lived in Comuna 13, one of the most stigmatized neighborhoods due to the scourge of violence and drug trafficking in Medellín. When I answered the call, the news could not have been gloomier: the planned visit to the Son Bata was called off because one of the boys at the forefront of the event, Andrés Felipe Medina, had just been murdered.

Upon hearing the news, I hung up the phone and began to weep. After a few minutes, I called General Naranjo, the director of the National Police and one of the government officials with whom I had developed a close relationship. When my appointment was announced, he was the first to reach out, sharing that he was also new to his role and assuring me of his support. We had always felt a strong empathy for one another.

I called him, tears streaming down my face, pleading for an explanation of what had happened. I needed to know if my decision to visit these youths had somehow contributed to this tragedy. Guilt consumed me, and I kept telling myself that I had underestimated the risks involved in my visit. General Naranjo responded gently, "Paula, if you take responsibility for these things, you will drive yourself crazy. We will investigate the case thoroughly. Please, be calm."

Like all the other members of Son Bata, Andrés lived in Comuna 13, an urban area in Medellín located in the mountains in the eastern part of the city. This area was mostly inhabited by migrants and state authority was absent. In the nineties, the place laid host to drug trafficking in tandem with an acute rise in hired killings, converting it into one of the most violent areas of the entire country.

A large group of Black men and women from Chocó, many fleeing the war and lack of opportunities in their region, arrived in Medellín and established their Palenque in Comuna 13. Most found work in construction, while others were employed as housemaids. They re-created the essence of Chocó in their new home, to the extent that one quarter of the commune is actually known as Small Chocó. It was here that these youths formed the group known as Son Bata. The name combines two words: "son," referring to flavor and rhythm, and "bata," a drum originating from the Yoruba tradition. Son Bata represented a small piece of Africanness—fledgling yet resilient.

The day Andrés was killed, July 24, 2010, was the saddest moment of my time as minister. I got ready and my closest advisers came to pick me up to go to the place where Andrés lived. First, we arrived at the place where the youths from the hip-hop groups had gathered. They occupied one of the main streets at the entrance and formed a circle of close to fifty boys, embracing each other. We joined the circle. Everyone took turns to say something. When my turn came, the only thing I could tell them, soaked as I was in tears, was that Andrés' death would not be in vain. I could not say more. It grieved my heart to see so many young boys engulfed in pain and hopelessness. As we stood there, a message arrived from the leader of the gang that claimed responsibility for the assassination, saying that the incident was an error by the one who was patrolling these "invisible boundaries" that evening, who, drugged as he was, had mistaken the target. Invisible boundaries are the territorial control mechanisms established by illegal gangs; a regime set up to cross from one quarter to the other at certain hours may lead to serious consequences or a required laissez-passer.

From there, I walked to Andrés' house. The police and military had taken up positions in anticipation of my visit; I could see and feel the presence of more than two hundred men gathered around, with trucks lining the streets. As we navigated the slopes covered with brick houses and zinc roofs, separated by makeshift narrow streets, we entered the small home where Andrés lived with his mother and sister in a single room.

Upon my arrival, I immediately clasped Andrés' mother to my bosom and hugged his sister tightly. His mother held my hand and guided me inside the room—a space without a window. The only source of light came when the door was opened. The floor was no more than six feet deep, creating a sense of confinement that mirrored their reality.

In this tiny space, she tried to reconstruct the final hours of Andrés' life. He hadn't been able to sleep the night before, eagerly preparing for my visit. He told her repeatedly that he had seen me at a distance during the concert and was excited to meet me. She recounted how, as early as five in the morning, he had prepared coffee, donned his best clothes, and declared, "Mom, this day will change our lives. I want you to come with us so that you can meet her." Her eyes were red, but the tears had dried, leaving behind a face deeply etched with grief. She stared at me with vacant eyes, both of us hoping that amid the sorrow, someone would emerge from the blues to awaken us from this nightmare, bringing Andrés back and revealing that it had all been a cruel joke. Andrés was her second son to be snatched away by the merciless fangs of violence. Thus, she was left only with her twelve-year-old daughter, in whom I could perceive the strength that she would henceforth be expected to give her mother.

During her trance, Andrés' mother kept saying, "She is the only one left," pointing to her young daughter, a beautiful girl with frizzy hair, who showed no tears, seemingly unable to comprehend the magnitude of what had happened. Just hours before, at five-thirty in the morning, Andrés had left the house to collect the sound amplifiers, ensuring everything was set for the occasion scheduled to begin at eight in Son Bata. Ten minutes later, two shots rang out just two blocks from their home. A few moments after that, a body was found lying prostrate on the ground, one breath away from death.

I felt like the most insignificant and impotent person in the universe. What could I say? I left the room, looking at the other houses above. I was imagining in which of them lived the assassin and what could really be going through his mind. Certainly, it was another youth without prospects who had mistakenly extinguished one more glow of light in that Comuna.

At midday, I found myself in church, having arrived as discreetly as possible, accompanied by the police and escort services. When they opened the coffin, I took Andrés' hand and whispered, "In one way or another, Andrés, we have met. Here I am." How I wished to see him with his eyes open, his hands in motion, to watch him walk, sing, and dream—to have danced with him and shown him my affection and friendship. Instead, I only knew him there, in that cold coffin. When he breathed his last, barely twenty-six-years-old, he had just begun working toward the creation of the national platform for violence and the celebration of the International Day for Peace.

Each time I meet a young rapper, my thoughts immediately turn to Andrés, and I find myself paying tribute to him, embracing the young artist as if he were truly Andrés. In its program, Visible Hands would focus on at-risk youth and hip-hop as a means of honoring Andrés. His death would inspire new life, ensuring that the premonitions he expressed in his songs would not befall others like him.

Back in Bogotá, I reminded myself that this death must not be in vain. The lives of youths like those in Son Bata need not to end this way. I reached out to Carlinhos Brown, my lifelong brother and renowned Brazilian musician, to help channel the pain felt by the leaders of Son Bata and transform it into renewed and fearless hope. I was convinced that his experiences with youth in the Brazilian favelas of Bahia, in contexts like Medellín, held the spiritual power necessary for this transformation. The leaders of Son Bata traveled to Brazil, and this show of solidarity became another significant highlight. Following that, Juanes, another dear friend and brother of mine, also met with them and has remained closely connected to their cause ever since.

I have closely followed the activities of these youths. Without a doubt, Andrés' death has not been in vain. Son Bata, along with other groups in Comuna 13 and various areas of Medellín, has defied violence with hope. Today they stand tall as examples of social transformation among youth. They have boldly continued to produce music and lead the resistance. Just as Andrés had expressed before leaving his house, he ignited in me—perhaps unknowingly—a passion to change the lives of youths like him and their families.

Chapter 25

The Last Day

After the elections, rumors swirled about the new cabinet, and many assumed I would be asked to stay on. But I knew my time had come to an end. I was exhausted, and the Ministry needed someone with fresh blood and renewed energy—someone who definitely was not me.

Several weeks before the induction ceremony, we began the handover process. In meetings with the team of the new president, Juan Manuel Santos, the tone was notably aggressive. Witnessing so many people anxious for power only reaffirmed my decision to distance myself from that kind of environment. The president had not addressed me directly during this time.

A few days later, I received a call from President Santos, requesting that I continue in my role. I told him I would prefer to discuss it in person. My hands began to sweat profusely, and I grew increasingly nervous. My primary concern was how to communicate my thoughts to the president in a convincing manner without closing any doors. I decided to reach out to several of my mentors for their opinions, and they all agreed it was time to step away. One of them asked, "Paula, what does your gut tell you?" My answer was a resounding no. He replied, "Then that is it. No." Additionally, I had just received a Fulbright scholarship to study at the Massachusetts Institute of Technology (MIT), and I was thrilled about it.

I arrived at the campaign headquarters of the president-elect, where he expressed his desire for me to continue as Minister of Culture for a few more months. I thanked him for considering me but explained that I had reached a point of exhaustion. After more than three years in the ministerial role, I felt I had lost sight of myself and needed time to recover. My final answer was that I would not continue, but I wished him all the best. I mentioned the document "Culture of Peace," which I had written for his team. Just as I had urged President Uribe to focus on diversity,

I suggested that peace should be the new priority—little did I know he had already chosen peace as his flagship initiative. I intended to convey my gratitude for his gesture. As I left his office, all eyes were on me, with various media agencies waiting for a statement. I sealed my lips, only smiling. I did not say anything to anyone until a few days later when the president-elect announced his new Minister of Culture.

President Santos took office on August 7, 2010. The event brought together national and international leaders and took place at Bolívar Plaza. I was no longer seated at the front but rather in the middle row. The weight of the ministry on my shoulders was now a thing of the past. From that moment on, I ceased to be defined by the post I had held. At the end of the ceremony, we were invited to the Casa de Nariño to congratulate the new president, who had transitioned from being a fellow colleague to now becoming the new boss.

On that day I returned to the Casa de Nariño. Compared to my first entry into that building, I saw everything differently; I was a changed person. I had woken up in a state of infinite tranquility, genuinely happy to step away, knowing that the next day I wouldn't wake up with a thousand thoughts juggling in my mind. Mission accomplished. I chose to wear a beige dress that shimmered subtly, topped with a white overcoat with high heeled shoes. I donned this elegant outfit not to impress anyone, but because it felt natural to me. As I walked along the red carpet once more, I felt like someone familiar with these corridors and their escape routes. I took the same elevator, this time free of yesterday's fears, unaccompanied by anyone. During those three-and-a-half years, I had entered unannounced, but that day I did not need to check myself in the mirror; I knew I looked good. The dress I wore was the right choice, and the pressure that once weighed on me was no longer part of me.

The ceremony came to an end. I had arranged for one of my best friends to pick me up at a nearby corner. As I sensed everything winding down, I moved closer to one of the entrances to say goodbye to the gentlemen who had been my escorts for three-and-a-half years. They all looked at me and asked, "Are we going with the new minister or with you?" I kissed and hugged each of them, thanking them for their support over the years. With a broad smile, I replied, "With the new minister."

They insisted on accompanying me, but feeling as if I had regained my wings, I bade them farewell and walked down the street alone, free from anyone watching over me. I arrived at the corner where my friend was waiting for me, almost running in my excitement.

I asked my friend if I could drive his car back to my house, and as I put on the seatbelt, picked up the keys, and turned on the engine, I felt like I was regaining my soul. Gripping the steering wheel felt like reclaiming control over my life. I didn't want to look back; my mind was set on the farewell party organized at my favorite discotheque, Pachanga y Pochola. When I arrived home, everything felt new, as if I had finally taken a moment to appreciate its beauty. I realized that much of what I had bought in those days was more out of zeal than taste. Now, I wanted to truly contemplate my surroundings in this place that had felt more like a hotel—merely a spot to sleep—than a proper home. I took my time to bathe, then dressed in blue jeans, low-heeled shoes, and a white shirt with a jacket before heading out.

At ten that night, I entered the discotheque, climbing the stairs and stepping on the beautiful black and white tiles. On the far wall, a giant screen displayed my photo, accompanied by words of congratulations. Waiting for me was Yiyo, the club owner and a close friend from my university days. As soon as I walked in, he played my favorite song: "Sin Negro No Hay Guaguanco" (No Blacks, No Swing) by the Lebron Brothers, a musical salsa dynasty from Puerto Rico. Deeply moved, I handed my jacket to a friend, raised a toast with a shot of liquor, and lifted my glass as we sang the chorus over and over, celebrating not only my tenure as minister but also my return to my true self.

Part VIII

Carpe Diem

Dulce sits before the camera, a radiant eleven-year-old from Medellín. Her large brown eyes hold depths of wisdom and a seriousness beyond her years. As I sit beside her, I tell her she might one day lead Manos Visibles (Visible Hands), the nonprofit I founded in May 2010, shortly before stepping down as Minister. She looks at me and firmly replies, "No, I want other things, different things for me. I do not want to do the work that you do, Paula." Her response is unflinching, and from our few encounters, I sense a beautiful consistency in her—a blend of depth, serenity, and clarity, like each strand of her long, twisted, thick, and radiant braids.

Dulce is a slim, five feet tall Black girl who lives in the comunas (slums) of Medellín. Her name, which means "Candy" in English, reflects her essence—joyful, beautiful, and sweet—but she is also serious. Weighing only seventy-five pounds, Dulce's words carry an unexpected gravity that captivates those around her. When she speaks, her presence commands attention, drawing us into her world, where every word resonates with meaning and purpose. Her gaze is steady; she listens intently, absorbing each word until the end. After her initial reply, I asked her what she would like to become. She tells me, a developer and psychologist, explaining that she hopes to help people's emotional health through technology. Then her eyes lit up as she also revealed her love for the sea, nature, and the cosmos. "I am fascinated by astronomy," she added. We were on the set of one of the main Colombian media outlets, launching a documentary about our project Naidi Valley, in which Dulce participates in the Women and Girls in Technology Program, a prelude for the fifteenth anniversary of Manos Visibles.

In Dulce's words, I sensed her determination to forge her own path. She projects a clarity that she is no less than anyone else and that her skin color does not define her possibilities, even in a society that sends a daily reminder that opportunities and spaces are limited for her, predetermined by others. As a member of Flor Púrpura, an organization dedicated to empowering Afro-descendant women in Medellín, Dulce is supported by a network that fosters both individual and collective growth by dismantling racist, sexist, and class barriers.

I met Erika Cruz, the founder of Flor Púrpura, in 2011 as part of the MLK Scholars program in Medellín when she was still a university student. Born and raised in Comuna 13—once deemed one of the most violent areas in Colombia and Latin America due to the presence of armed gangs, guerrillas, and paramilitary groups—Erika's journey has been transformative. She was one of the first manos visibles of Medellín, when we started our leadership programs for young women community leaders in 2013. Later, as a fellow of the 2017 master's program in public policy, her research focused on building a platform for Black women in the public sector, while also establishing her own organization to combat racial and gender inequality in the city. She worked for the local Secretary for Women and founded Flor Púrpura in 2018, led by five powerful Black women with the support of Manos Visibles.

Since the age of nine, Dulce has been part of a thriving community. Through Flor Púrpura, I have witnessed the initial seed grow into a flourishing garden, now encompassing more than three hundred girls and women, ages ten to twenty-eight. They confront a society steeped in racism and are igniting a revolution. From the margins and slums of Medellín, they are transforming the heart of a city that often fails to embrace its diversity, challenging the narratives surrounding Afro-Colombians—many of whom are born in the city but are perceived still as eternal migrants and victims of conflict.

For Dulce, at her early age, racial equality is not just a cause or an aspiration but an affirmation of her right to choose beyond the meaning that society has given to one of her identities, and to define her life purpose and a single direction for her journey, she has been prepared for it. She wants to break free from the confines of representation; she seeks to live her life without the burden of liberating or representing anyone. She does not subscribe to the myth of heroes or heroines. Her desire is both valid and liberating, shaped by the echoes of women like her in positions of power, naturally crossing various spaces over this last decade—the very decade of her existence. With a steady gaze, she looks at me and says, "Thank you for what you've done," yet her words carry no trace of idealization—what a profound lesson that is for me. Dulce, more than sweet, is a force of nature—a girl with eyes that seem to hold the universe, towering in presence, embodying the wisdom and leadership that have ignited my passion in supporting a growing movement of Black and Indigenous girls changing the paradigms for Black women in urban areas in Colombia.

One of the times we met was in the reading club of Flor Purpura, where we discussed the original Spanish edition of this memoir. As I prepared this updated version, I asked her opinion about the book. She inspired me to consider how this memoir rewrites itself as history evolves, giving rise to a new generation with renewed paradigms for the power of women, particularly Black women. She said, "I think it is a book about the beauty of difference, and I learnt to believe in myself, in my capacities and abilities being a Black woman. I know I am a visible power." She continued, "And also that the woman I admire most is Kelly Johanna Salas Asprilla—my mother. She is a warrior who, despite all her struggles, fights every day to provide for me. She strives to create a life different from her own, supporting my dreams and fostering my self-confidence." In that moment, I was transported back to the first chapter of this memoir, standing in front of a mirror that reflected my aspirations, frustrations, contradictions, and fears. As I find myself in the mirror of her eyes, I see a balance of my life and legacy, but the emergence of a new generation—unseen no more, bold and ready to claim their future. It is not any more a single vertical mirror but a room with multiple mirrors with multitudes of people reflecting on me. Some of them even became part of my iris, helping me to better control the lights and shadows that I have seen in my path.

I wonder if, when Dulce reaches my age in her forties, she will be as free as she dreams of being now. Will society, as she enters university and the workforce, have transformed enough to allow her to rise above racial bias? Will she belong without asking to be included? I hope so. My only solace is knowing that many of us have devoted our lives to making this utopia a reality for children like Dulce who deserve it. While I may not have all the answers now, I dare to believe—why not? Thousands of girls like Dulce have formed an intentional audience for my first and second books; through their reading, I reach out to summon the future.

Chapter 26

Charting Our Path

In the past decade, the rise of women—particularly Black women—into positions of power has become increasingly visible. From leading prestigious universities to serving as vice presidents throughout the Americas, including the United States, Colombia, and Costa Rica, and assuming ministerial roles in Brazil and Colombia, they are undeniably making their mark. But what does it truly signify? While symbolic representation marks progress, it often falls short of systemic change. Having one, the first, or even a few at the table is not enough in our collective quest for equality. What realistic expectations can we hold for this representation? Will it truly make a difference simply because we are present?

At the same time, a broader conversation is emerging around diversity, equity, and inclusion—now even incorporating accessibility, particularly in the private sector. Cooperation and development agencies are becoming more intentional in their efforts, working not just for ethnic communities but alongside them, recognizing these communities as key intellectual actors in shaping and directing initiatives.

This surge may be a fleeting moment, yet I strive to believe—and try to help create—a powerful momentum for generational change that can genuinely reshape the landscape of leadership and effective citizenship. We must envision a future where diversity is visible and normalized, rather than relegated to token exceptions that are celebrated and sweet in the short term but bitterly and poisonously attacked in the long term. This reality makes us acutely aware that even if the door is partially open, it will largely remain closed because we do not hold the keys. Some will continuously change the locks each time we configure to unlock them, or they will temporarily pass their keys, only to change the locks again soon after.

As of 2024, Mexico exemplifies a convergence of gender and democracy, marked by an election featuring all-female candidates and the nation's first woman president. Women now lead the Supreme Court, the Senate, and the Electoral Council, signaling a significant shift toward comprehensive representation across the country, propelled by regulations that prioritize gender equity.

However, this transformation raises critical questions. Having women in positions of power does not automatically equate to effective leadership, nor does it guarantee a diversity agenda driven by purposeful actions and a compelling vision—one that transcends mere titles to cultivate genuine influence. Yet we do not hold men to the same standards; it is this exceptional moment that prompts us to seek advancement for individual women, hoping these leaders recognize the countless years and the many women who have tried and failed in a society that often deems them inadequate, even when compared to their less competent male counterparts. Will they work from day one to ensure that other women can continue to forge paths until such representation becomes the norm? The years ahead will determine whether the burgeoning visible power of women in Mexico can catalyze the profound systemic changes we so desperately seek.

True representation transcends mere visibility. For Black women, representation has often been limited and dismissive of our multifaceted contributions worldwide. Many of us have been relegated to the margins, our stories overshadowed by dominant narratives that reduce our existence to mere stereotypes. This systemic invisibility has turned our identities into tokens, highlighting the urgent need for our societies to embrace our talent and capacity as catalysts for transformation. By confronting these inherent contradictions, we can pave the way for new futures that benefit us all.

In the United States, we recently witnessed history as the first Black woman vice president ran as a presidential candidate. Meanwhile, in Colombia, our current vice president—a Black woman, community leader, activist, and conflict survivor—was elected with the highest voter turnout in the nation's history. Her pivotal role in elevating the current president, a former combatant of the Guerrilla M19, is a moment I never imagined witnessing in my lifetime. Across Europe, particularly in the United Kingdom, Black women are stepping into leadership roles within political parties and parliament; however, the most visible among them are ultra-conservative figures supporting initiatives that stand against migration, minority rights, and historical responsibility. We must not assume that simply because we are Black women, our agendas will inherently align with liberation and transformative ideals. The presence of a Black president, Black vice presidents, or any political leaders does not guarantee a bold agenda focused on reducing inequalities or that resonates with our lived experiences.

This is a critical moment to chart the course of our collective journey. These political pioneers possess the freedom to navigate their power dynamics, yet we often wish for their actions to reflect the ideals they represent. There exists a level of freedom that allows for failure, a reality that challenges our expectations for them to achieve tangible results through service to all people. Women are increasingly aware of their critical role in shaping the future of healthy democracies, facing an ethical imperative to enact meaningful change in spaces laden with contradictions. The interplay of progress and backlash in this fleeting moment threatens to become ephemeral without tangible outcomes. It is insufficient to simply have individuals like us in power; when the individual story and ambition is prioritized over the populace, the boldness of agendas diminishes. Just because we are in these roles does not mean the outcomes will be different. Those in positions of power must embrace radical agency, wielding urgent and tactical leadership that transcends mere symbolism with a clear understanding of the converging crises that threaten humanity. Our identities should be a catalyst for a leadership that signals a clear agenda; boldness is imperative. We must harness this momentum to push open doors that remain tightly shut despite our initial entry. Now that some doors are ajar, we expect our leaders not only to remain inside but to leave them wide open for others to follow—and to change the locks, ensuring that future generations can enter and thrive in the places we fought so long to access.

Chapter 27

Unseen No More, the Visible

While we often highlight the political arena, there are other spheres that mold our perception and, consequently, our actions, especially the world of art. Art has long served as a foundation for transformative change; there may be no act more political than creating exceptional artworks that transcend boundaries and engage both traditional and unconventional audiences. Artists cultivate the resources needed for a future where we envision not just aspirations but also vibrant realities of social justice. Their creations illuminate pathways to address inequality, fostering empathy for the human experience and our shared dignity, as well as our limitless potential.

Yet traditional art systems and cultural institutions have often perpetuated the invisibility of diverse groups, particularly Black women artists and curators. This oversight has contributed to societal stagnation and shaped historical narratives that influence both the present and the future. Art canons have failed to capture the breadth and richness of diversity, especially Black artistry. Art history is a chronicle of our actions and cultures; however, Black artists often remain sidelined, overshadowed by familiar names, but Black artists have always been present, their contributions integral to the narrative. In this sense, we want Black artists to take their rightful place on the global stage to disrupt narratives and demonstrate the depth and breadth of their creative excellence that has previously been ignored, erased, or objectified. It is essential to illuminate the stories that exist among us and before us—stories that have been neglected—and to transform them into powerful, motivating forces. This realization inspired my journey to the Venice Biennale in 2022, where I participated in the Loophole Retreat, centered around the remarkable work of one of the greatest artists of our time, Simone Leigh.

CHAPTER 27

My first encounter with Simone's art was in 2019. After attending various events and meetings in New York, I took a day off to perform my ritual: a pilgrimage to Harlem. I wandered through the intersection of Malcolm X and MLK Boulevard, passing the Schomburg Center and stopping at my favorite spot, the Red Rooster, to savor some cornbread and admire their interior mural—its rich history and powerful phrases. Then I made my way to the High Line. There, in the distance along the avenue, I spotted a towering bronze bust of a Black woman, standing sixteen feet tall. Her commanding presence was timeless and transcendent; her braids captured my attention in a way that they are still being woven in my head. Moved from afar, I began to approach her, gazing from different angles. Each time I would draw closer, then step back, engaging in contemplation full of emotion, surprise, and joy. For the first time in a public space, I witnessed a monumental Black woman claiming her place in the world—solid, with a presence that was impossible to overlook, both ancestral and contemporary. It was a mama moment with *Brick House*, one the milestones of Simone's art in the world.

That image is etched in my soul, a profound reflection of my identity, embodying my grandmother, my aunt, and me—we stand tall, solid, majestic, infused with a deep sense of affection. I wanted to embrace the sculpture, to express what it meant to me. In that moment, even though I had never met Simone, I felt her essence become a part of me. Her art, intentionally diasporic, transcends time and borders, serving as a continuous reminder of the enduring strength and beauty of Black womanhood. Simone has not come alone; she is a mentor and professor within a vibrant network of intergenerational Black women in the arts globally. She lifts as she climbs, so when I received the news in 2022 that Simone Leigh was the first Black woman to represent the United States at the Venice Biennale, the largest and oldest international platform of contemporary art that hundreds of thousands (on average 800,000) visit each year, and that she had also called for the Loophole Retreat, inviting Black women in the arts from around the globe to gather in this historic moment, I immediately bought my tickets and requested time off from work, propelled by a deep aspiration to immerse myself in her world, to see more of her art, to listen to her insights, and to be close to the vibrant energy and community she emanated. I remember, when I registered, there was a long waiting list.

I was fortunate to attend not just as an individual but also as a program committee chair for the Ford Foundation's board of trustees, which was supporting both the retreat and the US Pavilion.

In 2022, I found myself at the entrance of the Venice Biennale, standing before the monumental *Brick House* surrounded by the works of extraordinary Black artists like Simone. She had claimed a central space in the visual arts world, and the overarching theme of her exhibition in Venice was "Sovereignty." She wanted to ignore the notion of nationalism entirely, instead emphasizing the self-determination of Black women. I love how Simone places Black women at the center transcending trauma to highlight autonomous acts of creativity. This approach not only redefines representation but also seizes the moment—carpe diem. During a conversation at the Ford Foundation in 2023, I asked her to elaborate on the key concepts of this central theme. She explained that embracing the idea of diasporic identity meant displaying the myriad ways we are interconnected, representing a group of women who are diasporic, and through the Loophole retreat, she wanted to respond to the idea that Black female intellectuals do not exist. I will never forget her remark: "Community comes with the artist, especially the intellectual community." She has been critical to open the doors not only for her but for multiple artists, allowing many of us to encounter the excellence and vitality of artists like Firelei Baez, whose work was behind *Brick House*, in an exhibition titled *The Milk of Dreams*. Firelei's pieces depicted oceanic, transatlantic, and simultaneously sidereal Black renaissance women traversing both water and the sky. At that moment, I had no idea that Firelei and I would soon cross paths at the Loophole Retreat. As I wandered through the Biennale, I was struck by seeing so many Black women walking around—a rarity in Italy. But Simone mobilized us from different corners of the world, to celebrate our art in the immersive environment of the Giorgio Cini Foundation. More than seven hundred Black women artists, curators, scholars, writers, filmmakers, and activists gathered from Nigeria, Brazil, Haiti, and a multitude of other diverse geographies of the African diaspora to celebrate the intellectual and creative life of Black women—our brilliance and excellence.

On the October 7, 2022, I boarded the vaporetto from Venice to a nearby island, eager to enter the sprawling multiwinged chateau. I yearned to connect with every woman present, even if most were strangers to me.

It felt like a constellation of remarkable trajectories, where the atmosphere buzzed with companionship and laughter, evoking the warmth of a family reunion. I sensed that there would never be enough time to fully absorb the inspiration each incredible woman had to offer; every story was a vital thread in the tapestry of my life's purpose. This is why I honor Simone and each of them in this memoir—an experience I will cherish for many years to come.

Rashida Bumbray, a powerful house voice for Black women artists, opened the Loophole Retreat with a tambourine in hand, singing a song from the South: "I've been to the river . . . Do you feel alright?" In that moment we became a community, a congregation gathered in a sacred space during a historic moment. The song served as a reminder of our collective call to action and evoked the legacy of Harriet Jacobs, who conceptualized the "loophole of retreat." This idea is drawn from Jacobs's 1861 autobiography, in which she recounts living for seven years in a crawlspace she referred to as her "loophole of retreat." This space was both an enclosure and a sanctuary for enacting practices of freedom—practices of thinking, planning, writing, and envisioning new forms of liberty. As Rashida sang, we all joined her in a chorus of joy and emotion. She is a beautiful Black woman and a powerful ally to Simone, embodying the spirit of community we aimed to cultivate. The three-day symposium featured dialogues, performances, and presentations centered on five conceptual frameworks: Modern Marronage, which refers to the communities formed by those who escaped slavery; Magical Realism, capturing the rich narratives woven from the music, literature, and movement languages developed by Black people in the New World in response to the traumas of colonialism and the Middle Passage; as well as medicine, sovereignty, and manual—pertaining to the hand or hands. Throughout the panels, these topics were explored through the intellectual depth and creative insights of more than sixty-five artists, scholars, and practitioners.

I vividly remember a break by the fountain outside the main auditorium when a tall, slim, young Black girl shouted, "Does anyone want a poem?" Her electrifying presence captivated us all, embodying the spirit of a new generation of artists and curators—many of whom were students or graduates of Spelman College, nearly half the audience. This moment resonated with the panel discussion between Simone and

Lorraine O'Grady, who expressed that she felt like she was "speaking to herself." They concluded that as Black women artists, they are not only creators but also are tirelessly working to be the ancestors of the future. In embracing this legacy, as Black women, we grapple with a short memory that often fails to fully register the depth of our experiences, our talent, and our intellectual force. These women have taken their rightful place on the global stage, disrupting narratives and showcasing the breadth and depth of their creative excellence—excellence that has been ignored, erased, or objectified for far too long. We were invisible no more in the art scene, actively forging the art archives of the future and challenging a universal canon that willfully omits our contributions. As I boarded the vaporetto on that final day, embraced by newfound friends, a part of me lingered behind, suspended in that vibrant moment, unsure if I had truly left or if a piece of me would forever bloom there.

Epilogue

Someone Like Me

In March 2018, as I approached the final phase of launching the original edition of this memoir in Spanish, I found myself in São Paulo for a global forum. On the last day, at around five in the morning, my phone began vibrating nonstop with a torrent of text messages. I scrolled through to find video clips, photos of mobilizations, and urgent press releases. Marielle Franco, an activist and politician, had been assassinated the night before in Rio de Janeiro, shortly after speaking at a forum dedicated to young Black women working to dismantle established power structures that oppressed them.

As sunlight streamed into my room, I felt an unsettling connection to her. Later that day, I attended a cultural event in a favela, where the entrance was adorned with ten posters drawn by children, filled with hearts and words of tribute to Marielle—the flower of the favela, la preta da Maré. Maré, one of Rio de Janeiro's largest favelas, is home to more than 130,000 residents.

At the end of the day, I received a poignant tribute poem from Anielli titled "She Died": "The Black woman of the tide has died . . . the woman who, once in the history of humanity, dreamed of justice, fought for freedom; precise was the shot, hitting its target with malice." It had been only twenty-four hours since her death, yet in that moment she was already being reborn within me.

Never had I witnessed such global mobilization surrounding the death of a Black woman—a queer from the periphery of Latin America. I understood the significance of leaders like Marielle, whose identity embodied intersecting diversities that compelled society to confront the layers of exclusion perpetuating its conflicts and inequalities. Amid the horror and tragedy, there was a silver lining: Marielle became a symbol of awakening—a movement uniting favelas, women, youth, Black and Indigenous communities, LGBTI groups, and a vast progressive global citizenship. She was a lotus flower flourishing in a swamp of segregation, perversion, and the contradictions inherent in our societies. By centering her work in the heart of these excluded communities, she bridged gaps in ways only someone from within could.

Marielle was someone like me—a Black woman in a position of power. I dare say she played an even more complex role, given her roots in the favela and the political stance she embraced. She ranked fifth among fifteen hundred candidates in Rio de Janeiro, becoming one of only fifty elected representatives, and the sole Black woman on the council. During her year as city councilor, she presented more than nineteen bills, two of which were approved. She was a formidable force, defined by her method and purpose. As a Black woman who rejected distinctions like parda, morena, or mulatta, she radiated strength with her loose, frizzy hair and colorful turbans. Her sharp, powerful gaze and radiant smile shone like the midday sun—illuminating yet casting a profound shadow. Marielle epitomized what I refer to as the "visible hand"—a leadership rooted in self-inclusion, one that is prepared, purposeful, and recognizes its own power while demanding effective equality.

This is precisely why I founded Manos Visibles (Visible Hands). I did not want to be the only Black woman in a position of power; rather, my aim was to contribute to cultivate a critical mass of leadership, organizations, and landmarks from the margins. My aim was to provide them with training, support, and strategic connections needed to materialize their vision and hopefully serve as agents of visible power and sustainable progress.

Over the past fifteen years, we have focused on the many visible hands of Colombian Marielles who have ventured into politics, alongside emerging artists following in the footsteps of our beloved Simone Leigh. Yet most of them are like Dulces, charting their own paths without the need to emulate anyone else—simply being themselves. Marielle's political spirit in Rio de Janeiro echoes in Milady from Buenaventura, now president of the local Chamber of Commerce. Marielle, the flower of the favela, is Erika, the founder of Flor Púrpura and a member of the Secretary for Women in the Mayor's Office, but there is also Katherin in Quibdó,

Brindis in Cartagena, and Maite in Tumaco. The LGBTI Marielle is Tania in Cartagena, founder of Las Libertarias, an association of trans women, while Kevin leads Matamba in Cali, and Álvaro advocates in Buenaventura. Name by name, I have witnessed the transcendence of their leadership—not merely as titles but as dynamic actions that have transformed the lives of hundreds and even thousands.

Over these fifteen years, more than twenty-eight thousand visible hands, from children to songstresses, have activated their leadership and harnessed their power for a country in dire need of their talent. The visible hands have emerged in diverse spaces, seamlessly integrating the ethnic diversity of Colombia across various sectors and levels. Our goal has been to create opportunities to enhance diversity within traditional elites and diverse sectors in Colombia from filmmaking, to literature, economics, technology, or public health with a network of dedicated national and international leaders, companies, universities, and a range of committed stakeholders.

In 2010, Visible Hands was nothing more than an idea nurtured by my cousin Patricia and two friends armed with three cell phones and two laptops in Bogota. Our "boardroom" was often a coffee shop or Skype, as I was studying in Boston at the time. As my tenure as a minister concluded, I asked myself: What next? I needed to re-create, reinvent, and ask myself what it was that made me happy. I noticed that the rightful answer to this question lay in the hands, hands that mold, hands that draw, hands that mark, hands that caress, hands that sow, raised hands, not begging or stretched out hands, hands with clenched fist and hands with open palms. That's what I wanted to do, to find these invisible hands to generate a form of visibility based on their identities as an asset and on the consciousness of their beauty, of their merit and based on their technical, ethical, and poetic potential. These visible hands have instilled in me a belief in visible power: the power of difference, the power of unconditional and inexhaustible humanity—a humanity where you are in me, and I am in you. Ultimately, in this shared humanity, we can always find in the mirror someone just like ourselves.

When I founded Manos Visibles, I envisioned a future where those of us fortunate enough to have opportunities would sow the seeds for the next generation. These past years have served as a launchpad for individuals—those who have stepped into diverse spaces, generously handing over keys and leaving doors open for others to enter. Over these fifteen years, we have proclaimed:

- We are not a separate, not "the other" Colombia; we are Colombia's future.
- We are not a deficit, a setback, or an eternal problem; we are a possibility, and you need us.
- We have shown that "minorities" can become majorities.
- We have ignited dreams once thought extinguished and impossible.
- We have demonstrated that diversity is not merely a concept but also a visible reality.
- We have transformed "no" into "yes," dismantling excuses along the way.
- We have navigated through joys, sorrows, and uncertainties.
- We have changed lives, families, and communities.
- We have faced the contradictions of power and asked ourselves: Now that we have it, what do we do with it?
- We have rowed against the currents of prejudice.
- We have opened spaces, declaring that every place belongs to us.
- We have kept doors ajar, even when they threaten to close again.
- We have loved a country that does not love us back and have committed to love it even more.

You may be wondering, dear reader, why I chose Dulce, Simone Leigh, and Marielle to close the updated version of this memoir. In the past six years, these three women have embodied a visible power, a power that challenges the invisible power that inspired the title of this book. Colombia, Brazil, and the United States have all been pivotal in my work on culture and racial equality, and I wanted to honor this new generation in Colombia while expressing my gratitude to these countries. I did not know a better way to pay tribute than writing about women who have inspired me, and as I reflect on their journeys, I see my own story mirrored in their smiles—the many reflections they have imprinted on my life.

When I received the news that, after knocking on so many doors, my memoir would be translated into English, I looked back—something

I don't generally do—and saw how much has changed. These years have led me into a new life. In these complex times, we are called to redesign, rethink, retool, and redream our goals, equipping ourselves to reanimate, redirect, and anticipate the challenges that lie ahead in such a pressing and intense present.

We are still invisible in many spaces, but in recent decades, as never before in history, there is no doubt that Black women are more visible in academia, in the media, in the public and private sectors, and are leading most of the racial equity agenda. The big question that remains is whether this has translated into broad societal well-being at the scale we need. This book is an invitation to the new generation to work for more equality, but with more tools, so that the content is a new impulse for transformation, channeling the experience of the current generation that is shaping the future and trying to accelerate progress. The increased representation and visibility of Black women in power is not just a story of relative success; it also is a call to action. Together, we can create a future where diversity is celebrated, and every individual has the opportunity to flourish.

For me as an author, this memoir is part of my legacy to this world and a tribute to more than twenty years of work for racial equality in Latin America. I believe in the power of writing to reverse so many absences and limitations, to raise new levels of consciousness, to build ourselves in other ways.

Acknowledgments

I extend my deepest gratitude to those who have illuminated the path of this translation. The first spark of belief in the importance of this work came from Gilbert Ndi Shang, who, in 2008, translated the book shortly after its publication in Spanish and authored a literary review that affirmed its profound resonance with diverse experiences, challenges, and realities around the world. In 2024, Ana Isabel Vargas joined this journey, weaving rich contextual layers to connect with an international audience. Together, Gilbert and Ana have provided unwavering support, helping me see the transformative power of sharing this memoir beyond Colombia's borders. Their dedication has preserved the essence of my Colombian experience, the richness of linguistic diversity, and the ongoing pursuit of equality within these pages.

I am also profoundly grateful to those who have amplified my voice over the years, particularly Darren Walker and Henry Louis Gates Jr. Their thoughtful engagement with this manuscript has reaffirmed its significance, both now and for future generations—especially for those striving to forge legacies in uncharted fields and geographies.

My sincerest appreciation goes to Michael Millman at the University of New Mexico Press. From our very first conversation, he embraced the vision of this project, becoming a steadfast ally in shaping this updated translation for today's readers.

This book is born of a tapestry of experiences spanning over twenty countries and fifteen years, beginning with my tenure as Minister. I documented these moments in a diary, later immersing myself fully in writing during pivotal periods, including my SPURS/Fulbright Fellowship at MIT (2010–2011) and my time as a World Fellow at Yale (2014). In 2024, I found refuge at the Bellagio Center of the Rockefeller Foundation, where

I completed this translation and authored a new chapter on the power of women—especially Black women.

I am deeply grateful to the institutions and organizations that provided me with the time and space to reflect on these experiences. Their support has allowed me to shape a legacy of equality and cultural power that this book now seeks to share with readers in Colombia and around the world.

About the Author

Paula Moreno *is a Colombian industrial engineer with a Master's in Management Studies from the University of Cambridge, along with further studies in urban planning and leadership at MIT and Yale University.*

Her leadership has made history in Colombia, where she became the country's youngest and first Black woman to hold a ministerial position. Internationally, she has been the youngest and first Afro-Latina member of the Ford Foundation's Board of Trustees, where she also chaired its Program Committee. As the founder of Corporación Manos Visibles, a leading NGO working for racial equality in the Americas, Paula has irrevocably touched the lives of more than twenty-eight thousand people, primarily Afro-Colombians, and contributed to the creation of more than five hundred community-based organizations over the past fifteen years. Her work has expanded to eleven countries, building cross-border programs to support Afro-descendant populations worldwide.

Recognized as one of the world's most prominent Black leaders, Paula has earned numerous honors. These include the Unita Blackwell Award from the National Conference of Black Mayors in the United States, the MIPAD recognition from the United Nations, and the UK Black Excellence Award. She has also received the Order of St. Charles from the Colombian government and the Order of the Aztec Eagle from the Government of Mexico. The Council of the Americas selected Paula as one of the region's most influential young visionaries, and the World Economic Forum has celebrated her groundbreaking social entrepreneurship for racial equality. She has received the Fulbright Excellence Award and the Global Fairness Award. Most recently, the Skoll Foundation named Paula Moreno one of its Fellows and the Rockefeller Foundation as one of the Bellagio residents.

Beyond her professional achievements in academia, public service, international cooperation, and philanthropy, Paula's talents extend into writing and cultural production. She has been a columnist for *El Tiempo* for more than a decade and is author of two books, *El Poder de lo Invisible* (The Power of the Invisible) and *Soñar lo Imposible* (Dreaming the Impossible), both published by Penguin Random House. The first chapter of her second book has been adapted in the Netflix series *Maria La Caprichosa*, and she is executive producer of music albums and films. Her multifaceted legacy has grown in power and influence, serving as inspiration for young leaders, women, and ethnic communities across the Americas and beyond.